Mantra
Repetition in the Land of Alzheimer's

Denise Weeks

This account is drawn from my memory of events. I have changed the names of everyone involved in my mother's care except for my own, my husband's, and my son's. I am eternally grateful for all the care my mother has received from these named and anonymous helpers.

ISBN: 9781549670978
Imprint: Independently published
mantra.Denise.Weeks@gmail.com

To Patty Girl

Wanderer, there is no road;
the road is made by walking.
By walking one makes the road,
and upon glancing behind,
one sees the path that never
will be trod again.

Antonio Machado – "Campos de Castilla"

CONTENTS

PREFACE

When your parent with memory loss starts repeating the same story over and over again, you hope it's going to be a good one. The story that ended, "No Sean, that man does not have his penis on your head" was a winner. We could sit back and smile when she started in, appreciating the narrative arc and the physicality of her telling. It was short. It packed a punch. It had unlikely genitals. And it evoked a rich and content time in my mother's life. The one about her stepmother's damp girdle, the only item that survived when she and her brother accidentally set the clothesline on fire, was also good. It had villains, heroes, even foreshadowing. She could tell that one over and over and always get a laugh. But the story whose climax was, "Grandma, she's a doozy of a dog!" always left me cold. Some repetition is endearing; some can only be patiently endured.

Every story about Alzheimer's is a story about repetition, a coming back, over and over, to what has been lost, what has already been said, and to questions about what we can't know for sure: how long the disease will last, what it will take next, how it will all end. Though decades of research have now plotted out the disease's typical trajectory, and many of its sufferers

1

will pass by the same well marked milestones, how and when people progress from one stage to the next cannot be accurately pinned down. Will my mother live 10 years after diagnosis, or 20? How long will she know my name? Will she lose language before the ability to walk? What will be the exact cause of her death? No one can say for sure. Genetics; baseline physical, psychological, and mental health; environmental factors; stress; falls; diet and exercise; the will to live; chance. Each of these will do its part to create a unique path for every sojourner. "The road is made by walking," and no two travelers will walk the exact same path. In that way, paradoxically, there is less repetition in Alzheimer's disease than you might expect.

This story recounts my mother's and my first six years on the journey into Alzheimer's. During the one-year period it took me to write this book, my mother remained relatively stable. Maybe it was that stability that gave me the breathing room to look back at where we'd been, consider all we'd been through, and take stock of where we were. And writing was a useful outlet, a constructive way to make use of all the repetition. It's meaningful to me that I did not write this account entirely from hindsight but rather as it was, and still is, unfolding. Some of the earliest challenges (car, credit cards, caregivers) are resolved, but many of the themes present from the beginning—her strong independence, her unresolved childhood issues, her love of ice cold beer—persist. Is it repetition when we go over this ground again and again, or is it as T.S. Eliot puts it in his poem "Little Gidding," "to arrive where we started and know the place for the first time"?

The stories here are my mother's and my own, but perhaps more mine because I'm the one noticing and recording, and I've been present in this tale since its inception, from those first niggling observations of loss and the earliest slips and changes. I often wonder what it would have been like if my mother had lived far away from me during the first few years of the disease, out of my gaze, just as I wondered, when I was pregnant, what it would have been like if I could have started my journey toward motherhood already six or seven months along. That would have trimmed it up a bit, and it would have allowed me to skip all that early noticing, all those comments on my size and weight and looks, that would, under normal circumstances, be downright rude. Same with early Alzheimer's. The early noticing is not the most compassionate, especially when what you're noticing is so mundane and, frankly, inconvenient. Missed walking dates, forgotten events, and all the repetition. If I had not come on board till my mother's memory loss was much greater, maybe I would have jumped straight to compassionate caregiving and skipped irritated scorekeeping all together. We would have skipped many unhappy discussions about what she did and didn't need, what was or wasn't wrong, and why I should or shouldn't be so involved, but without that basic training in endless repetition, I might not be as prepared as I am now for what lies ahead.

The books I enjoy most on this topic are those that do not whine but also do not sugar coat the pain and frustration involved in caring for someone with exceptional needs. Some of these include *The Glass Seed* by Eileen Delehanty Pearkes, *Her Beautiful Brain* by Ann Hedreen, *Mother in the Middle* by Sybil Lockhart, *A Bittersweet Season* by Jane Gross, *Life with Pop* by Janis Abrahms Spring and Michael Spring, and Atul Gawande's *Being Mortal*. From these I have been happy to glean useful tips and read about others' moments of enlightenment. I enjoy those moments best because they're presented like a sacred lotus: beautiful on the surface of the water but thickly mired in the mud of painful experience just below.

That is not to say it's all pain and suffering. My way on this journey has been bolstered by the help of my husband and son; by the monthly support group I attend for adult children caring for a parent with dementia and my friendship with that group's leader; by the incredible work of our local Alzheimer's Society and our community's Adult Day Health program; by three dedicated caregivers who've come on board over the years; by a friend and email pen pal with whom I've had a near-daily correspondence for the last 15 years; by yoga; by long walks in the forest; and by my dog. I mention these resources here because of their tremendous importance. At each stage of the journey, different kinds of help and information become necessary. You won't need every resource I've listed right away—though it's never too early to find a support group and never too late to get a Corgi—but by about one or two years in, you'll want some variety of all of the above. All and possibly more. The parent you care for may still have a healthy spouse; you might have willing siblings; you might belong to a strong faith group with built in caregiving functionaries; you may have helpful neighbors. Use them all, and not just once. And maybe find in this book and others like it another kind of valuable companionship, a confirmation that you're not alone.

In a way, this book is everything I would have said at support group if I could have hogged the floor each month, talking rapidly about all that had gone on since the last meeting. Ninety minutes a month for five or six years running might have been enough time for me to share all that's contained in these pages. But then, leaving no time for others, I never would have heard all the stories that gave me hope, taught me lessons, and made me laugh. Stories that I have shamelessly borrowed and repeated here. No, instead of taking all the time at group to share my reflections, I've put them down here. All that's missing is the box of tissues and laughter.

1. SHE'S A DOOZY

Before I became my mother's caregiver, I was in the early stages of an interesting new relationship with her called "neighbors." We hadn't ever lived in the same town as adults, so like many mother-daughter relationships, ours had been conducted in the hopscotch manner of visits, phone calls, and letters. But then the birth of my son coincided with my mother's retirement, and she figured, why not? She moved from California to Bellingham, Washington, where we had just moved, into a sweet house about half a mile away from us. We were neighbors and "newbies" together, exploring what Bellingham had to offer and finding shared, but also separate, interests. Of course my son was the main reason she followed us up the coast, and our relationship also had this new component. She was growing into her new role as a grandma as I was getting used to mine as a mother. The steady, repetitive patterns that emerged from our new roles and proximity served all of us beautifully, for a while.

Much later, in a darker and confused time, when Alzheimer's had taken much of her independence, she'd sit in her darkened living room and tell me she wished she'd never moved to Bellingham, that she hated it there. She'd look at me with glassy, challenging eyes, angry and lost. I knew not to believe her. I knew that what she hated was the disease, even if she never called it by name. I knew she longed for a mythical wholeness, some vague "before." Maybe she said it to hurt me a little, too, because of how I seemed to be a part of what was happening to her.

But well before we got close to that time of pain and regret, my mother was anything but angry. She played a central, happy role in my son's young life: watching him several afternoons a week, picking him up from preschool, gathering him up at the bus stop through fourth or fifth grade. She was the classic loving and involved grandma, making treats, encouraging his artistic pursuits, sharing adventures, hiding Easter eggs, and, like many grandmas do, mourning every year that passed, wishing he would remain just like he was, right up until he was about 10. After that, it all got a bit hazy.

When she moved here she had an older dog, a sweet and intelligent Maltese that died suddenly and sadly in 2001. Soon after that she learned about a breeder of Bischons up in Vancouver, B.C., who got a return, a dog who'd been flown across Canada and then flown back because it hadn't melted its new owners' hearts. Turns out the dog spent most of its first year crated, in a garage, and its pitiful barking turned the insensitive owners off. My mom drove up to meet the little reject, a female named Zoey, and fell in love.

Who can remember every detail of an event, an occasion, an acquisition, a loss? At least one person, apparently, is burdened with something like the opposite of Alzheimer's: an ability to recall nearly everything that happened to her since she turned 14. And there are others with slightly less oppressive playback mechanisms who can, given any calendar date, tell you what happened on that day complete with dialogue, weather, and wardrobe. Me? All I know is that the dog was small and white and neurotic. I remember my mom and her new dog sitting on my back deck, and my son, a big talker, discoursing on how tired the dog appeared. A photo of the day jogs my memory. My mother looks happy and the dog is indeed sleepy—eyes closed and head down, possibly shutting out the stimulation of its new surroundings. What I recall, and my son says is true, is that he said something like, "That dog sure sleeps a lot. She's a doozer." A photo doesn't record words. We don't know if that's what he really said, but we know he was talking about the dog's generally soporific nature. My mother was tickled, as good grandmas are by their grandchildren, and she decided to change the dog's name from Zoey to Doozy.

Doozy was a terrible dog. One suspected that she either wanted to get back to Canada, or maybe get farther away from it, so frequently did she escape from my mother's house and take off running. And though small, she was not slow. She ran. She ran and ran, disappearing from my mother's house over and over again. Bellingham is a mecca for off-leash dog walking, but Doozy had to be kept tightly leashed or else she'd take off at her first chance or charge every easy going dog along the trail. Walking this 12-pound dog was a way to build forearm strength; you had to constantly restrain her from her ridiculous darting attacks. While other dogs frisked and sniffed, my mom would pick Doozy up to keep her from inciting a riot, and then she'd explain the dog's behavior with its name. She's a Doozy all right.

What does the dog whisperer say about aggressive dog behavior? That it's usually the human's fault? To be fair, Doozy came with a lot of problems, but my mom didn't spend much time trying to undo them, either. At the risk of overanalyzing, I do think it's worth considering: why was my mom's first dog, pound for pound no bigger than the second one, so relaxed and confident and such a trustworthy off-leash walker, while the second dog was such a neurotic menace? Is it unreasonable to wonder if something in the owner's confidence had changed?

My mom got her first dog when she lived near San Luis Obispo, California, while working as a mental health counselor. Divorced and on her own since her mid-40s, she had a job she loved, close women friends, a comfortable condo a few miles from the beach, and regular or seasonal visits from two of her three children, my older sister and me. My visits always included long walks on Pismo beach, hikes up Madonna Mountain, visits to the Thursday night Farmer's Market, or adventures farther afield to Hearst Castle, to Santa Barbara, or San Francisco. One summer when I was still in graduate school and not in a relationship that would make spending so much time with my mom a second-best option, we took a road trip up the west coast and across the Puget Sound to Victoria, British Colombia, camping and staying in cheap hotels along the way. I'd play and replay the cassette tapes I'd made of Kate Bush, Leonard Cohen, and Tchaikovsky, and she gamely endured them. At Oswald State Park in Oregon, where wheelbarrows sit near the parking lot so campers can haul their equipment the quarter mile into the campground, we woke in the night to torrential rains and the sound of other campers packing up and fleeing. What we did was dig a deeper trench around the tent and go back to sleep. The next morning, I couldn't get my mother to take a break from trying to make her damp "squaw wood" catch fire (plus she always prided herself on only having to use one match), so I walked to the beach on my own and assumed that we'd break camp and drive to the nearest town for breakfast. Instead, I returned to my mother smiling smugly over a blazing fire as she heated toast in the skillet. She was not one to back down from any kind of challenge, and she rarely looked for the easy way out.

When she visited me in Austin, Texas, our visits were similarly filled with outdoor activity of one kind or another. One spring I borrowed a bike for her so we could ride from East Austin over to Laguna Gloria on the west side, then down south of the capitol to have some Mexican food before heading the five or so miles back home. After seating us at our table the waitress asked my mom, who was beet red and dripping sweat, if she was okay. "No," my mother said dramatically, using handfuls of napkins to wipe her forehead, "My daughter is trying to kill me." On another occasion we set off by bus to the far side of town so that we could make a cross-town trek back, but after about 8 miles with many zigzags and too many miles to go to make it back in time for the dinner party my roommate had planned, we caught a bus. As it was getting dark, in a part of southeast Austin I didn't know, the bus driver, having just observed that we didn't look like we were from that part of town, told us we'd have to get off, that this was the end of his run. Encouragingly, he told us where to watch for the next bus but advised us to stand in front of the church while we waited, explaining helpfully that we were less likely to get shot on the church steps than near the road.

Anything that went wrong on an outing became fodder for our tales of adventure. There was the time my mother and I hiked through a field in Mammoth Lakes, California, and she had me help her onto the back of a grazing horse who stood still for about five seconds before darting purposefully out from underneath her, leaving her gasping for breath on the hard ground before she could finally force out, "I can't believe I tried to talk you into doing that!" There were the multiple occasions when outings got derailed by stray dogs that needed rescuing, and there were countless incidents of us getting in over our heads in one way or another. But typically, only one of us ever complained, and it wasn't my mother.

She didn't grumble much about Doozy, either; nor, despite my frequent criticisms, did she ever embark on a program to retrain her. She simply repeated the dog's name, as if that said it all: she's a Doozy of a dog.

At some point, I can't say exactly when, my mom started telling passing strangers the dog's name and then attributing the Doozy line to my son. Her story, neat and compact, went like this: "She came with another name, but after I got her and she did so many bad things, my grandson said, 'Grandma, she's a real Doozy of a dog.' So I said, 'That's it! That's what I'm going to name her.'"

What family doesn't have a story that gets trotted out over and over, despite its supposed actors objecting to how they've been cast? Who accepts outright the tales told by parents and grandparents of things we said or did in youth? And then there's what we know about memories themselves. Each retelling lays down the tracks for future telling, each recollection making the grooves deeper, more consistent. How the telling itself becomes the memory, erasing what might have actually happened, neatly eliminating complicated contradictions, making the story tidier and more certain.

As the Doozy story gained traction, my mom was gradually, but noticeably, losing her footing. Maybe this is why I hate the story so much. It reminds me of the beginning of the end of my mother's memory. There was no going back to set the record straight; there was only the forward journey through repetition and loss.

The first note I have of her failing memory goes back to 2006. I wrote in a journal that my mom didn't think her doctor was taking her seriously when she said told him she was worried about forgetting things. What I noticed around that time was that she was beginning to withdraw from some of her activities. After she moved to Bellingham in mid-2000, she joined the local Senior Center's hiking group, became a hospice volunteer, helped at a soup kitchen once a week, canvassed for the Democratic party, and later, volunteered at the Humane Society's consignment store and started taking a weekly yoga class. By 2007 or 2008, she stopped taking hikes, saying the group went too fast or too slow, that there were people who talked too much or didn't talk to her at all. She got offended that a hospice client asked her if she'd seen a ring that went missing but wouldn't stand up for herself or ask for another client. There was something she didn't love about the work at the kitchen, and it all became "too boring" at the consignment store. She lost touch with her more politically active friends, and later she stopped going to yoga because she didn't like that one of the other students asked her for a ride.

My son, by then in the third grade, didn't need quite so much babysitting, what with art classes and other activities that kept him busy after school, but she still had a couple afternoon shifts, days she'd meet him at the bus and take him home. One time she waited for the school bus for a full hour, thinking it would come at 2:00 instead of its actual time, 3:00, and she got upset. I didn't record every episode of her forgetfulness during those early years, but they began to be more noticeable.

What do we want to be our story? How do we explain ourselves? My mom cast her slow withdrawal from activities as dissatisfaction. They were boring. The people weren't nice. She was wrongly accused of stealing. I did not know the truth of these accounts, but I felt the results. She started closing herself off to new opportunities and I felt the pressure of being her only friend. Our walks together, still frequent and ambitious, began to feel more like a duty than the adventures we used to enjoy. I wanted her to stay active, but I also wanted her to have her own friends. Instead, she developed a Jekyll and Hyde routine: she became a friendly chatty Cathy on every walk, stopping strangers and telling them the story of Doozy's name, but at home she insisted she enjoyed being alone and refused any kind of help or organized activity. That was her story and she was sticking to it.

Now might be a good time to share a few of the tips I picked up along the way, tips that apply to this earliest stage of the journey. One of the best pieces of advice I received was to go to all of my mom's doctor's visits with her and to take notes. That's tip number one. Get a notebook and write things down.

11

The notebook I have begins in 2010, at the visit with my mom's GP following up on the neuropsychological evaluation she finally had after four years of thinking that something was going wrong with her memory. I know I went to doctor's appointments with my mom before that, but without notes—I hadn't started keeping a notebook yet—I remember very little. I do know the doctor she was seeing in the lead up to the diagnosis, and just after it, was determined to rule out everything he could. This is what a geriatric specialist should do. That's tip number two. Get a doctor, a geriatric specialist, if possible, who will methodically rule out other problems that might stem from cholesterol, high or low blood pressure, thyroid, vitamin D levels, blood glucose, low B12, and basic mobility (Parkinson's, Wernicke-Korsakoff syndrome). He did that, and my mom looked good on paper. But her short term memory was getting shorter and shorter.

Tip number three: keep going, and when the GP or geriatric specialist is out of ideas, or has too quick an answer, schedule a neuropsychological evaluation. My mother had hers at least a year after scoring 26 out of 30 on a mini-mental state examination (MMSE) screening at the Alzheimer's Society, after a bit more "ruling out" with her geriatric specialist. (Tip number four: go ahead and ask for an MMSE or similar screening. These cannot be used to diagnose the disease, but they give clinicians a baseline for future evaluations.)

The results of my mother's neuropsychological evaluation, combined with her doctor's evaluation and the thorough "ruling out" process that goes hand in hand with everything that gets figured in, were enough for the geriatrician to make the official diagnosis of "probable Alzheimer's," which, despite the big lead up in time and emotional energy, didn't surprise any of us. More generally disappointing than the diagnosis, perhaps, was the geriatrician's view that there was not much more we could do. He dismissed the efficacy of the current Alzheimer's medications on the market, but eventually prescribed Namenda, though he told us its benefit would be negligible.

My mother, the one who had felt for years that she was losing her memory, did not break down upon hearing her diagnosis. Not then, not later, and not for the five years since then, has she ever connected the word "Alzheimer's" to her experience. So you might wonder what the point of going through all the testing is.

When new people show up at support group, they're always advised to get their parent evaluated right away. Find out what it is. "Probable Alzheimer's" is not always the answer, and in getting a different diagnosis, some will learn very important information that changes the course of treatment and might require more specialized care. Some will learn that their loved one has signs of Lewy Body dementia or frontotemporal dementia, diseases that will respond differently to different drugs (and poorly to some commonly prescribed for Alzheimer's), or that an underlying mental illness has become aggravated, or that there are signs of other brain disorders: swelling from a fall, degeneration caused by strokes, damage caused by alcohol or drugs. Some might get what everyone at support group would consider a golden ticket: a diagnosis of a possibly reversible condition, something brought on by a simple urinary tract infection or a treatable metabolic imbalance.

Whatever the diagnosis, if you are just beginning to give care, this is a vulnerable time. Tip number five: If you use a computer, limit your time on the Internet.

Two or three years into the Alzheimer's journey, thanks to countless Google searches, I had read about the magical curative powers of blueberries, coconut oil, anti-inflammatories, coffee (at very high doses), ketone bodies, ginkgo biloba, crossword puzzles, etc. Talking to opinionated acquaintances, I heard that Alzheimer's was due to pent up anger, to not working through emotions. I heard that I could stave off the disease by changing my routine, even embracing inconveniences—a tip made, coincidentally, by someone given to being late and causing inconveniences. Following more credible sources could prove disappointing, too, because while research keeps coming up with more effective tools for diagnosing the disease—using gene sequencing, analyzing cerebral spinal fluid, doing more brain imaging, for example—it is hard to get excited when you're past the diagnosis stage and are hoping for something that will halt the disease or cure it all together.

But it's not all bad news, at least not for my mom. The mantra that has become popular in Alzheimer's care is, I believe, what has helped her the most: "What's good for the heart is good for the brain." Diet, exercise, low stress, social support. Everyone comes to the disease with a different set of skills and strengths, a different baseline in physical and mental health, a different life history. All of these will play out in the disease. My mother had walking on her side. Always a walker, strong and fit and still able to walk as far as I could on our twice-weekly outings, my mom was doing well by her heart. All except for the beer.

At a stage in the disease process when she could still vacuum, do laundry, and prepare some simple meals, surprising gaps in her personal narrative opened up. She forgot that she'd won a car one lucky day in the late 80's; she didn't remember that she'd had a black cat named Gita for a good chunk of the 20 years she lived in California. One day she asked me if she'd ever been a jilted bride. Nope. But for all that, she still had pretty decent basic math skills. We could test these skills around her constant inquiry into the wellness and age of my husband's father, "the Judge."

With unrelenting consistency she asked, "How's the Judge?" for years, nearly every time we got together. The Judge probably became a fixture in her imagination because of his generosity and kindness. He included her in all the family dinners he hosted when he lived in Bellingham before moving back to Houston, and he invited her on a family trip to Ireland to attend his grandson's wedding. The Judge is a noteworthy specimen. Still working into his 95th year, he has southern charm, stature in the community, and an old fashioned kindness for store clerks, bakers, and newspaper vendors. Also, he gave my mother someone to inquire about.

When she started asking how old the judge was, my husband, tired of answering and always joking with my mom anyway, started answering 135, 128, 115. Most of the time she said, "Stop kidding," or something to indicate that she knew that was impossible. But sometimes she'd say, "Really?" She'd wear us down in the asking and eventually we gave the real answer, "91," then "92," then "93," and so on, every day, every year, still counting. Her closing remark on the topic has always been, "Bless his heart," the verbal equivalent of a pat on the head.

Sometimes Paul has answered her question with a simple math problem. "He's 100 minus 7." My mom would pause for a second then ask, "He's 93?" He'd prompt, "You're 80 minus 3." Pause. "I'm 77?" Before Christmas one year she repeatedly asked me how many people were coming for dinner. After answering several times I started slowing down and giving names, letting her add them up on her own. "Mary and Derek," I'd start. "That's two," she'd say. "And Holly and Jeff and their two girls." Pause. "That's six." With more names and more pauses she arrived at the correct answer, 12, every time.

But when it came to beer, all bets were off. Counting was crazy making. My mom was like a militantly stubborn Karl Rove, insisting that we might be entitled to our math, but she was entitled to THE math. If she bought a 12-pack of beer on Tuesday, and on Wednesday there were only 4 left, she could not possibly have drunk 8. If she had 2 in the refrigerator on Thursday morning and bought another 12-pack that afternoon, but only 4 remained on Friday morning $[2 + 12 = 14; 14 - X = 4]$, that meant . . . But no. It never did. It couldn't. She insisted she didn't drink that many. No matter what the store receipts showed, no matter how many beer bottles were in her trash can, no matter how the refrigerator filled then emptied of brown Alaskan Amber bottles, she swore she only drank two or three beers a day, tops.

To tell this story is to summarize and possibly minimize a much greater, and sadder, problem. Everyone comes to Alzheimer's disease with a lifetime of habits or patterns of being that will work for or against them as they enter this period of decline. My mom brought alcoholism. Or maybe the alcoholism developed at the early stages of the disease, before I was paying attention to her grocery store receipts, when she started feeling vulnerable and alone. Or maybe she'd been drinking more heavily than I knew since my father divorced her 30 plus years ago. Maybe the incident that I'd understood to be an isolated event—the time she was sent home from her hospital nursing job because someone smelled beer on her breath—wasn't such an aberration after all. Maybe her good cheer and adventuresome spirit never entirely made up for the heartbreak she felt after being left, or maybe it went much deeper than that, down into the well of pain she experienced as a child: first when her mother died, leaving her feeling like an orphan; still later when her father remarried and she became the unloved stepdaughter; later still when her father committed suicide. Maybe she had never worked through those devastating emotions. But the more pressing question, post Alzheimer's diagnosis, was what to do about it.

In support group one night, a new member—whose father had the disease and seemed, from her telling, to be a very self-conscious participant in his decline because he could talk about it, observe it, and mourn it—said that it was important not to "over-catastrophize" the situation. Not to say that "the sky is falling" too soon or too often. It will fall, sure enough. For now, it's sufficient to observe that it's raining, so get an umbrella and deal with it. I liked that.

The question every caregiver asks—asking it every day, many times a day, over the course of many years—is, "what next?" Or maybe, when it comes to driving, living alone, writing checks, not eating, or drinking too much beer, the question has to be, "what NOW?"

When my mom called, not infrequently, to ask us if we'd seen Doozy, we had to enter the "what now" mode and leave "what next" for later. The good news was that Doozy always turned up. We'd find her in my mom's backyard or around the neighborhood; upstairs in a closed room or under heavy blankets on my mom's bed; or, when my mom still drove, sitting in the car. On one occasion, however—and here I'm jumping ahead to when my mom was no longer driving, but don't worry, I spare no details in the telling of that saga—Doozy didn't show up in any of the usual places. In my best approximation of search and rescue, I set out in the car, driving the route my mom usually walked, intending to ask the cashiers at the store she normally went to if they'd seen the dog.

I knew to ask this because after she became car-less my mom's habit was to walk to the store pulling a pink, two-wheeled cart with one hand and Doozy, on a leash, with the other. (If you happened upon her making this journey, as many friends and neighbors within a two-mile radius reportedly did, you'd see her hunched over, head down, face set, hair wild, tugging her uncooperative dog each step of the way. You wouldn't see this duo and think, "Now that's normal.") I also thought to check at the store because my mom always enjoyed telling us how much the cashiers there adored Doozy. Every time she shopped, my mom reported happily, the cashiers asked, "Where's Doozy?" and begged my mom to bring her in. When she did, according to the story, everyone stopped what they were doing to violate health and safety codes by standing around petting the dog. Another story she told featured Doozy making a brazen escape from her collar and wandering in to find my mom at the meat counter. "There I was when Doozy walked right up behind me. The man behind the counter smiled and asked, 'Is that your dog?'" That Doozy.

On this particular day, when I set out on my search, Doozy had not attracted such loving attention. She had not escaped her collar to follow my mom to the meat counter, and no cashiers had asked my mom to bring her cute little dog inside. Instead, Doozy had been left outside, tied to the trash can near the entrance, where no one noticed her looking in expectantly every time the doors whooshed open, and no one, not even my mom, gave her a second thought on their way out. I didn't need to ask the cashiers anything because before I got into the store I found Doozy standing there, surprisingly calm. She looked, for once, like she had no wish more dear to her heart than to go home and stay there.

Dog found, mission accomplished. With that rather surprising "now what?" taken care of, with all its implications for just how forgetful and distractible my mother was becoming, it was time to think about "what next?"

2. ALL IN THE TIMING

When you begin your journey on this path, whether as a caregiver or a patient, you often wonder, "What's normal?" Magazines ranging from *AARP* to *Men's Health* reassure us that it's normal to lose your keys occasionally, to take longer to recall a name (if you were ever good at remembering names), or to forget your pin number at the ATM. As we begin to notice these lapses we either share or hide them from each other, depending on our confidence and mood. Asking, "Have you seen my glasses?" can become an endearing routine. Patting yourself down in a frantic key search can become a signature move. But having to admit, "I must have forgotten to pay those bills," or routinely coming home from the store without the milk you were sent to buy will begin to raise eyebrows. It's natural to want to hide these foibles or rationalize them away. "It's nothing. I was just distracted." Blaming is handy, too: "It's your fault; you should have been more clear."

For my mother, living alone made these lapses easier to hide. No one was counting how many times she walked into a room, forgetting what she went in for. No one watched as she put drinking glasses in the cupboard where the plates usually went, or stashed mail into her address book. She probably laughed at herself when she found socks and underwear in the linen closet. If she spent hours a day looking for her purse, who knew? And even when she began to worry, as she did four years before she was diagnosed, what was there to say? All she had were the flimsy and malleable stories of loss and inconvenience that pointed to a truth she did not want to accept.

My mother had no good way to explain how she left Doozy at the grocery store. On its face, it didn't compute. Where was her attention? Where was her muscle memory? Where was she looking when she walked through the doors and right past the dog who must have been looking up at her, probably barking that high pitched, nervous yip she let out whenever she wanted attention? With no good explanation for it, this disturbing new information was simply discarded. Within minutes of my returning from the store with Doozy in hand, after telling my mom where I'd found her, the anxiety and self-recrimination my mom had expressed seemed to drain away and were replaced by relief and a maddening "who me?" innocence. As a caregiver to someone with dementia, you learn that blaming and explaining are, at best, pointless, but it's hard, especially in the early stages of the disease, to resist looking for teachable moments. "Look mom," I said, trying to build a watertight case, "Here's a reason you shouldn't walk to the store with Doozy anymore." I suppose I hoped that she'd respond with a look of equal parts sorrow and recognition, a look that would tell me that she understood. I wanted her to see it as I saw it. I wanted her to see me: a daughter, acting quite reasonably, trying to help her mother. What she saw, instead, must have looked a lot like disloyalty, or worse, cruelty. Why couldn't I just leave her alone? Her face admitted nothing but annoyance.

What daughter hasn't spent a lifetime trying to read her mother's face? As communication between me and my mother started to break down, I had to rely more and more on guesswork. Sometimes I thought I could see something telling in the set of her lips or the way she moved her eyes sideways, looking at me then looking away. Anger, frustration, or something she wanted to say to me but couldn't, or wouldn't. Had I been better at this in the past? Didn't I used to know, nearly telepathically, when she thought something was funny? Didn't we used to simply exchange a glance and know what each other was thinking about that rude sales clerk, the bearded man blowing smoke rings, or the skinny lady with the big hair? Sometimes we'd have to avoid making eye contact, fearing that we'd break into the inappropriate laughter I remembered from mornings in church as a Catholic school girl. Forbidden laughter, probably another sin, seemed more hysterical than any other kind. But now, trying to figure out my mother's moods and motivation had become difficult, and my struggle often boiled down to one impatient question: Why couldn't she just say what she felt?

Applying the crystalline vision of hindsight, I can see that my mother and I were on two entirely different tracks. Mine was the path of stubborn insistence that things could go on the way they'd always been, that I could push and prod my mother toward a greater open mindedness (or at least to seeing things my way), where each new shared experience would lead to increased closeness and deeper understanding. Her path, meanwhile, was turning more and more toward a different kind of status quo. How could she get from here to there without drawing attention to herself? How could she ward off unwanted inquiries and interrogation? I wanted her to reflect on what was going on, while she wanted to downplay the significance of what was happening. My refusal to understand the signs of that early decline seem obtuse now, but in my defense, I can pause at the word "happening."

Alzheimer's comes on gradually. "Insidious onset" is the actual medical term used to describe it. Research suggests that by the time someone begins to show outward manifestations of the disease—far beyond "normal aging," and a step or two past "mild cognitive impairment"—when activities of daily living begin to be affected, the disease has already been at work disrupting neuron transmission, eroding the hippocampus, attacking various regions of the brain for up to a decade or more. Since everyone's brain is different before the disease, it follows that everyone's brain will respond differently to the decline, even as generalizations can be made about what to expect as the disease progresses. If my mother had what I critically labeled a bit of a "martyr complex" long before the diagnosis of Alzheimer's—a perpetual "I'm fine" insistence even when she wasn't, an expression of "Oh, go on, enjoy yourself; I'll just sit here and eat a worm"—how realistic was it of me to expect that in the face of such terrifying potential loss she'd become forthright and gain the ability to speak her mind? Her mind was becoming less and less familiar. Better to just avoid looking too closely at it, she must have thought.

It is not uncommon to hear at support group that the dementia sufferer "puts on a good face." This happens a lot around doctor's appointments, trips to the store, visits with long-lost relatives. The on-the-ground caregiver will have seen numerous slips in daily functioning, will have experienced jarring exposure to memory loss, will have noted bald evidence of decline, but in front of a stranger, the one with dementia will "present" quite well. "She seemed perfectly normal!" the caregiver says later, incredulous.

In these situations the caregiver feels stuck between two bizarre and irreconcilable realities. To tell the doctor or store clerk or relative, "This is not how she is at home; you should have seen her yesterday!" feels like a hateful outing of a person quite happy to live in the closet. And besides, does the store clerk need to know that your mom can't find her checkbook nine times out of ten as she stands there writing her check like any other shopper? Do we keep track of every incident of forgetting so we can make a case for how our loved one "really is," or do we let them have a few minutes of dignity and independence? It often feels like a no-win situation, where keeping track is the path of attachment—counting, spying, wallowing in loss—but allowing my mom to sit there and tell the doctor cheerfully, "No really, I'm fine!" is the path of aversion—putting on blinders, rejecting the hard truth.

Shortly after my mother's diagnosis, well before she left Doozy at the store, I helped my mom switch doctors. The original geriatric specialist she saw was skilled in his craft but not a good fit for my mom. Polite, decorous, nonintrusive, he didn't probe deeply into anything she reported, leaving her feeling, even with her "no worries, I'm fine" defensive shield, unheard. I helped her change over to an ARNP, an Advanced Registered Nurse Practitioner, who'd been recommended by a few people at support group, and the difference was immediately clear.

Erica came into the room and looked at my mom directly, spoke with volume, and asked lots of follow-up questions. After a few visits, the three of us settled into a comfortable routine. Erica would ask my mom how things were going, if she had any pain, if she'd had any falls, and then she would ask my mom if it was okay for her to ask me those same questions. It was such a respectful way to navigate the rocky shoals. "Is it okay if I ask your daughter?" It was in those three-way conversations that we would eventually get to the topic of my mother's drinking.

"What about alcohol. Are you still drinking beer?"

"Oh, occasionally."

"How many beers are you drinking a day?"

"One or two."

"Is it okay if I ask your daughter that same question?"

With that opening I could share with Erica the byzantine mathematics of my mother's drinking problem, and though my mother would interject that she never drank that much—she couldn't possibly have had seven beers—many of these visits ended the same way: Erica would tell my mom flat out that what she was doing was opening a bottle and "drinking memory loss," and that she was going to end up falling and having to move into a home. She had to stop. My mom would get teary at some point, admit that drinking had become a problem, and vow to quit. And she'd quit. For a day or two. Maybe a week. But at some point she'd start again, and I'd be back to my vigilant counting.

During one of these cycles, at an office visit when Erica shared something about her Irish heritage and commiserated with my mother about a story my mom had just told about her difficult childhood, Erica suggested that my mom see the center's counselor. That my mother agreed was a pleasant surprise. Did she really just admit that she wanted to talk to someone about what was going on? I felt humbled. Maybe it had been unrealistic to think that my mother would open up to me, but look, here she was, ready and willing to talk to someone else. Sort of.

My mother had three sessions with the counselor before she announced one day, in a tone equivalent to brushing dust off her hands, "That was nice." She was done with counseling. She was still drinking and was, as far as I could see, in as much denial as ever, but, she said, she had told the counselor her whole life story and really enjoyed it. What else was there to say? She didn't want to take any more of the counselor's time and had cancelled all her future appointments.

I shared the story of my mom's three counseling sessions at support group one night, thinking that my mom's reluctance to examine what was happening to her—her aversion to intro-spection—was a universal symptom of the disease. But I learned that some of the parents being cared for talked about their experience of loss openly, and felt it keenly, and were even busy getting their affairs in order because they under-stood where they were headed. None of that was true for my mom. She expressed her biggest admission in language like,

"I'm losing my mind," or "I'm getting confused," or "You know, I'm forgetting things," but she never used the words that went to the root cause. Despite the excellent discussions she had had with her ARNP and counselor, she seemed unable to connect what she was experiencing with the notion that she had a disease called Alzheimer's, and that it was progressive, but that she didn't have to face it alone.

Instead of using her counseling sessions to discuss her Alzheimer's diagnosis and the loss that it entailed, her fears, her coping mechanisms, or her drinking, my mother used her sessions to repeat the story of her childhood, a story whose skeletal outline got told often during those first years of the disease. Her telling always combined a bit of an "it's fine" bravado with a poignant intensity she'd add by catching the eye of the listener and holding them with a look that undermined her levity.

"My mother had tuberculosis," she would begin, then tell how the family had moved from their Eagle Bend, Minnesota, farming life to urban Phoenix, Arizona, where her father started working for the railroad. They were a family of five when they left Minnesota: George, her father; Florence, her mother; Kenny, Florence's son by a previous marriage; my mom; and Jimmy, my mom's younger brother. Within a few years, by the time my mother turned 7, they were a family of three. Her mother had died, despite the supposedly healthful benefits of the desert heat, and her father had given Kenny away to a childless couple down the street. Having been traded for a pig at some point in his own young life—or bartered long enough, anyway, to work off the debt his family incurred in acquiring the pig—my grandfather must not have thought this such an unusual arrangement. A widower, taciturn, and given to depression, he was ill equipped for fathering two young children. He hired babysitters to watch my mother and her brother when he worked, and the babysitters would lock my mother and her brother outside all day in the Phoenix heat while they entertained their boyfriends inside.

A series of negligent caretakers came and went, each one embedding in my mother's psyche a feeling of being an unloved orphan girl: someone who could be cast off, rejected, "put out," and forgotten. But then one day, another kind of woman answered my grandfather's ad, one who had another skill set entirely. Recently out of the convent, militaristic in her discipline, and skilled in the kitchen, she whipped that sad little household into shape. She came into their lives like a commando, my mother would recount. One night she made a delicious roast beef dinner with mashed potatoes, and shortly thereafter my grandfather asked for her hand in marriage.

"Imagine!" my mother would say, "Here we were, two wild children, barefoot, with dirty clothes, when Mary came along." All that kept Mary from being the classic wicked stepmother was her own sad back story. Born in Mexico, smuggled into the U.S. after her own mother died, she entered the convent as a way to escape from poverty, where she hoped to be educated and become a teacher. Instead, she was put to work in the kitchen for many years and was unhappy enough there that she coordinated an escape with the help of some other kitchen staff while the rest of the nuns, always required to travel in pairs, watched a movie. Her escape brought her back to Arizona and into my mother's life, where she played a part in nearly every other sad story my mother would tell about growing up feeling unloved, unseen, and unappreciated, a Cinderella story without the fairy godmother.

At some point, when I availed myself of the services offered by the counselor on my own, seeking ways to deal with my mother's continual drinking, the counselor said something to the effect of, "Your mother has been very hurt, but she is strong. She's not likely to ever admit that she needs any help."

I knew my mother was strong willed, and I knew she'd suffered. It helped to hear from a professional, however, from someone who sees much more of this than I do, that my mom was unlikely to change. Had she really used the word "ever"? As in never ever? And yet. How long did I keep hoping that my mom would wake up one morning and tell me what she needed? Then I could get off her back, I'd rationalize. She didn't want me hovering and interfering, and I certainly didn't like her being evasive and withdrawn. I see now that what I wanted was for my mother to become self-actualized, while what she wanted was to have her freedom. And she wanted it ice cold.

Walking to the store was her ticket to freedom. The beer she bought there was . . . what? Evidence that she could still make her own decisions? More forgetting? A soothing balm?

My son's high school wrestling coach has a gesture he makes. Holding his fists out in front of his body, extending his elbows to the sides, making a circle of his arms, he says, "Circle of control, boys, circle of control." The wrestlers cannot control what the opponent looks like, how big he is, or how fierce looking, but they can control their own behavior inside the ring. Lots of things are beyond our control, he says, so just stay focused on what is in the circle rather than getting distracted by everything outside of it.

What lies within the caregiver's circle of control, I often wonder, and what's beyond it? To rephrase the Serenity Prayer, how do we know the difference between the things we can change and those we can't? Where does that wisdom come from? Unfortunately, a lot of the wisdom in knowing the difference comes from trial and error. Before that, from books, handouts you can pick up at the Alzheimer's Society, and from tips and insights you get at support groups and other people's stories. At every stage of the disease new issues emerge, so timing is also an important factor. What works for one period of time might not work just six months later. Sometimes we try a new strategy and it fails—not because the strategy was flawed, but because we were too early in applying it. The advice to not "over catastrophize" can really help caregivers relax and wait before rushing in to "fix" things, but it doesn't mean that we should avoid getting ready to do so later on. Keep limber; stay alert. As Eisenhower said, "In preparing for battle I have always found that plans are useless, but planning is indispensable."

My first attempts to "take control" of my mother's noticeable losses of motivation, socialization, and general orientation to what was going on around her failed miserably. I contracted with an agency to send out a caregiver who could provide company and take walks with her on days I couldn't, or, more honestly, didn't want to. I imagined that with more activities and distractions, she'd be happier and would drink less.

At that point in the progression of the disease, my mom was far enough along that she could forget that she had actually agreed to allow someone to come over, but she wasn't so far along that she could be cajoled into letting them in when they came to the door. And then, if they did get past her first resistance, she'd prove how little she needed them by suggesting they take a five-mile walk and trying to wear out her so-called helpers. A hallmark of the Alzheimer's diagnosis is an impaired ability to acquire and remember new information, but everyone who cares for someone with the disease can cite the odd assortment of fascinating new facts their loved one picks up, retains, and retells till you'd prefer the exile of Ovid over having to hear it again. After this initial foray into outside caregiving, my mom's favorite new story became the one about the caregiver who couldn't keep up with her. "She was a little heavy, and I could see that she was out of breath. I said, 'That's okay, we don't have to walk all the way to the lake.'" That caregiver only lasted a few weeks.

Sometimes I had to wonder about the interplay of my mother's memory and machinations. The woman was a little heavy, yes, but as far as I could tell, she was a fine walker. But the story, the way my mother told it, worked so perfectly to her own advantage. It showed that not only did she not need someone to walk with her, but that she was the one providing the care. That poor woman, my mother got to say. She could barely walk! Long after the experiment had failed, I heard that story at least three times a week, possibly for up to a full year. Later, when I eventually took courage and was ready to try again to find someone to spend time with my mom, she had the story at the ready: "But only if the person can walk. One time I had this lady visit me who was a little heavy, and she …" Yes, mother. Only if she can walk. Sanity through repetition. Keep it simple, agree when you can. Try not to take the failures personally.

This was my punishment for getting the timing wrong and interfering too soon. I had provided my mom a handy argument to use against me. But given all that she was losing and had already lost, how could I begrudge her this new story— and its hundreds of retellings—that cast her as the strong one, the one leading the way?

3. NEW NORMAL

It's normal to want to remain as independent as possible for as long as you can. A person suffering from Alzheimer's is no different from anyone else in that regard. What isn't normal is the hyper vigilance required of those who take on the role of caregiving. It's not normal, but suddenly it's a way of life, the new normal that keeps evolving.

To remain vigilant is stressful, to say the least. To wonder what upsetting news every phone call might bring or to worry every time you knock on your mother's door—not knowing what you might find inside—is draining. The unfortunate combination of wanting to "solve" every problem that presented itself and not having much of a Mother Theresa-style dedication to the sick set me up for one frustration after another.

One of my favorite studies on the stresses of caregiving compared the recovery times of caregivers to non-caregivers. Both groups had a plug of skin removed—just a small bit, nothing gruesome—and then the subjects' healing times were recorded. No surprise, the subjects already stressed by the burdens of caregiving healed more slowly. Caregivers have been shown to be at higher risk of depression, sleep deprivation, high blood pressure, digestive problems, obesity, and other ailments caused by general and unrelenting stress. Books that focus on tips and strategies for caregivers outnumber books on the disease itself, for obvious reasons: our current health care system, even our national economy, cannot do without us. If we don't take care of ourselves and stay the course, who will care for the millions of people in the early and middle stages of the disease who could not live semi-independently without our help?

Diagnostic techniques for identifying Alzheimer's disease keep changing. When I started educating myself about the disease and its course around 2009, I read a chapter from a book called The Atlas of Alzheimer's Disease by Howard H. Feldman titled "Clinical stages of Alzheimer's disease." This chapter discussed seven stages that chart the progression from "normal" to "severe Alzheimer's disease." Normal, in case you're wondering, is defined, "At any age, persons may potentially be free of objective or subjective symptoms of cognition and functional decline and also free of associated behavioral and mood changes." Note "may" and "potentially." In other words, you might be "normal" and still be moody as hell. At the seventh stage, when the disease is labeled "severe," "AD patients require continuous assistance with basic activities of daily life for survival." The breakdown of function and the estimated amount of time a person will spend in each of the seven stages makes for grim reading. Language skills, ambulation, the ability to sit upright, the ability to swallow. All are lost in the last stages of the disease, if the person lives long enough.

I would like to see a similar clinical breakdown of caregiving. Not a study on what happens to caregivers, but what actually constitutes giving care. Who gets to call themselves a caregiver? What does the mantle really mean?

The support group I attend is for adult children caring for a parent with dementia. That means all forms of dementia—Lewy Body dementia, frontotemporal, vascular, Parkinson's related dementia—not just Alzheimer's disease. "Adult children" is self explanatory. But what about "caring"? Some of the people who come to group live with their parent or have moved the parent into their home. Some are attending to parents who live in other states; they fly out to visit two, three, or six times a year. One woman comes down from Canada to care for her mother who lives in Bellingham, our town 30 miles south of the border. Some of the parents we care for still live in their own homes. Of those, some are still married to a healthy spouse, often the caregivers' other parent, and some are with partners who have medical conditions of their own. Many of the parents being cared for live in assisted living, a memory care unit, or in skilled nursing facility. To say, "I care for my mother who lives in her own home" every month, as I do when we go around and introduce ourselves at the beginning of each meeting, is to claim what, exactly?

A diagnostic tool for identifying stages of caregiving, similar to the diagnostic tools we have to identify states of dementia, might read something like this:

Stage 1: Normal. You accept the basic humanity of your parent. Yes, you notice that he/she forgets to replace light bulbs, where the keys are, what she came into the room for. You notice those things more if you live with the person. You have no idea how often they occur if you don't, but you're not counting yet anyway. "Normal" in this stage is normal in the widest possible sense, taking in every kind of natural dysfunction families can and will produce. Your mother may be insane, but if she always was insane, that still counts as normal.

Stage 2: Noticing. You don't have a designated notebook for writing down the slight disturbances you see because you're not a writer or you're not obsessive (yet), but you begin to notice things. You get irritated at your parent, and you feel mad at yourself for being so impatient, but there it is. You may or may not share this observation with siblings or friends. If you have infrequent contact with your mom or dad, you might chalk these incidents up to "a bad day."

Stage 3: Please!, Short for the "Please use more Post-it notes" stage. While the person you're noticing might be moving from Mild Cognitive Impairment (MCI) into the next stage of the disease, your thoughts run to solutions. If only the person would write things down. If only they'd call to check in more often. If only. "Caregiving" in this stage can be broadly defined as making lots of suggestions for ways the person can stop forgetting.

Stage 4: Help. At this stage, you see that Post-it notes aren't cutting it and you turn to worrying, blaming, and hair pulling. The lapses you're seeing are consistent enough to warrant some investigation, but you find that point-blank questions don't get you very far. You start to encounter some resistance, against which you naturally push back. At this stage you might discover that while arguing isn't actually helping, you continue to argue and explain things very rationally because it's all you know how to do.

Stage 5: Stepping up. Unless you are the very distant child or one of many siblings who allows others to do the work for you, you start to do more than make suggestions. You start to do stuff. If you're plugged in to resources, you start to educate yourself about what to do next. By virtue of worrying and spending time reading and talking to others, you are giving care. What follows from this might be going to doctor's appointments with your mom or dad, looking into their finances (are bills getting paid? is credit card debt piling up?), and, inevitably, starting to look ahead.

Stage 6: Donkey work. If you ever felt like you would rush in with one good idea and solve the problem, that time is past. Now you realize that there is no "saving." Staving off repeated disasters, real or imagined, is the nature of the work, and it requires an ongoing, relentless, repetitive commitment.

Of course there are many more gradations on the caregiving continuum. The family that takes in an aging parent to live with them gives more care on a daily basis than the daughter who flies out to visit four times a year. These are not trivial differences, though they don't address what worry and concern and paperwork might be going on from a distance. So there are differences. But what I've noticed at support group is that most people, by the time they've started coming to a support group, don't see any need to compare. They understand that what works for one family might not work for another. This is lesson number one in good support group etiquette: you can share your experiences, but you don't tell other people what to do. We each find our own way. If it works out that you can, or maybe have to, for financial reasons, have your mom move in with you, and you're still sane after 20 minutes, then yes, that might be just the thing. Some caregivers get their loved one into some kind of assisted living arrangement early on in the disease process, while others wait for the emergency that forces their hand. Some who give care are not sure what's best and try out various arrangements before they find one that works, but it might only work for a little while. At the next critical turning point in the need for care, the one who gives it has to start educating themselves all over again.

What's "normal" in the context of caregiving is that at every stage in the progression there will be a shift from "normal" to "new normal" to "next new normal" till you stop counting. It's no longer business as usual, if the old usual was to not have to worry about what your mother was up to at any given moment. The way we move forward doesn't have to include looking for catastrophe where none exists, or, as Wendell Berry puts it so beautifully in his poem "Wild Things," we do not need to tax our lives with "forethought of grief." No, but it helps to be pragmatic.

For example: I didn't react hysterically when my mom mixed up the bus schedule and missed meeting my son after school one day. He survived. I continued to ask her to meet him there once a week, but to be safe, I got him a house key, just in case. I didn't demand that she turn over her car keys after she picked me up from the hospital where I'd had a minor surgery, when, on the way home, she stopped several times in the middle of various intersections because she wasn't sure where she was. But following that unsettling incident, I made sure to circumvent any opportunities she had to drive my son anywhere. Is this serenity? Circle of control? To accept the things we cannot change, but to come up with plans B, C, and D.

When my mom walked to the store with Doozy and came home with a 12-pack of beer but no dog, I made the pragmatic decision not to ask my mom to watch our dogs when we were away, even for an afternoon. She always offered to help us out in any way she could when we traveled, and watching the dogs had been fairly simple. Does it seem odd that I continued to let her watch my son once a week but not my dogs? By that time my son was catching on, and could probably fend for himself, I figured. The dogs, not so much. It didn't make sense to risk having our older dog and our new puppy end up being tied to the trash can in front of the Lakeway Market. It wasn't a good idea for an afternoon, and it was out of the question for a multi-day trip.

I could not halt the progression of my mom's disease, but I could try to eliminate preventable disasters. I still might "wake in the night at the least sound / in fear of what my life and my children's lives may be," to borrow more of Wendell Berry's words, but I would keep my dogs safe. In this temporary new normal, that was how I could work within my circle of control.

4. LIES

During toasts at our rehearsal dinner, my soon-to-be father-in-law said of his son, now my husband of twenty-plus years, that he never knew Paul to lie. I couldn't imagine a more affirming reassurance that I'd chosen wisely. Though ours is not a perfect marriage, it is true that none of our complaints have to do with dishonesty. As parents we try to instill in our teenage son the higher path of truth telling when fibbing, evading, and boasting seem to provide the easier out.

Even in yoga the topic of truth comes up. *Satya*, a Sanskrit word translated as non-falsehood, is the second "great vow" that one commentator, Swami Satchidananda, puts on par with the superpowers of any decent action adventure hero: "With establishment in honesty, the state of fearlessness comes. One need not be afraid of anybody." Who wouldn't want that? Who doesn't fantasize about that better version of him or herself who never has to worry about what others think but faces every moment with a strength born of clarity, transparency, and simplicity—those other inspiring words we associate with truth? The yoga commentator goes on: "When there are no lies, the entire life becomes an open book." If that's so, then the life of a person caring for someone with Alzheimer's is more like a locked journal wrapped with duct tape stashed under the mattress hidden in a padlocked room. Lies, lies, lies.

In caring for my mother, I find myself telling more and more lies. Some are lies of omission, like not telling her how much I pay the caregivers she insists she doesn't need, while others would have the lie detector needle jumping wildly, graphing falsehoods that range from matters of finance to matters of freedom. "No, this program doesn't cost anything; isn't it great?" "No, I haven't seen your car keys anywhere. They must be lost." It's a question that always comes up at support group: new caregivers see a chasm opening up before them, where speaking the truth is difficult, at best, but lying seems even worse. They'll ask how to navigate this rocky ethical terrain, and experienced caregivers advise, "Just lie."

Acting in what we believe to be our loved one's best interest, we lie to get things done, to ease anxiety, and to spare ourselves the pointless repetition of lengthy explanations. Over time, and as a kind of consolation, we come to learn that lies can, in fact, be more kind hearted than many of our truths. Instead of answering the question "Have I already told you this?" with an exasperated, "Yes, at least ten times," we practice, "I don't think so," or, "Maybe, but tell me again." We can lie by invoking the authority of the doctor, claiming that "the doctor said you need to do this" when it's time to unplug the gas stove, put on a First Alert bracelet, or tape down the area rugs. We might lie in the old bait and switch way, inviting the fearful parent out to lunch and then mentioning, on the way, that first we have to stop and get some lab work done.

One of the most profoundly compassionate lies I ever heard was from a woman at support group who had dedicated years to caring for her mother with Lewy Body dementia. Splitting shifts with her husband—between them spending upwards of four hours a day visiting, trying to calm her mother's "firestorms," running interference with the nursing home staff—Annie told of the time she got to her mom's room at 4 p.m., her regular visiting time, only to encounter her mother's blind rage. "You're late!" she screamed. "I've been waiting here for hours!" To her mother's angry outburst, Annie abandoned the surface truth and replied with a much deeper one, answering simply, "I'm sorry."

That story has always been a reminder of one of the greatest truths in caregiving for someone with dementia: we don't have to be right. Telling the truth might seem like the higher path, and being right feels good, but the outcomes are what really matter. Is the person who receives your care getting their needs met? Are they safe? Are they finding meaning in their much diminished life? These are big enough challenges. Trying to orient them to reality, whatever that might entail in any given situation, is asking too much. However dangerous it feels to admit this, especially with a teenage son and my own strong urge to tell it like it is, or at least how I think it is, I have come to see that in caregiving, truth is contextual at best. A few facts can go a long way; sometimes it's better to dole them out slowly over time, or rearrange them, or simply keep them to yourself.

And yet. A big part of the struggle I've had caring for my mother through the early years of this disease has been the artifice that has grown up between us. I'm not talking about the inevitable reversal of roles, of daughter becoming mother, of mother becoming the child. I'm talking about all the pretending. Pretending to be interested in the fifth repetition of a story. Pretending it's perfectly normal to find a plate of cooked food on the bookshelf. Pretending, for her sake, and using her words, that "she's fine," that yes, everything is "great." Pretending not to mind that she can't engage with me on the emotional realities in my life. Pretending to know what I am doing. I often think that perhaps the best training for caregivers would be acting or improv school. We could be taught useful facial gestures and body language; we could be fed effective lines; we could be drilled on how to marshal our energy to get us through the 2- or 4-hour performances. Maybe if we looked at it as acting, it wouldn't be so hard.

Good caregivers, of course, the caregivers we imagine we could become if only we had a few more injections of saintliness, remain fully themselves and are naturally compassionate, well equipped, and infinitely resourceful. They stay in the present moment and can always be counted on to give kindness, as caregiving guru Wendy Lustbader exhorts in her rousing presentations. I have met some of those. And, sadly, I am not one.

I may not excel in the aspects of caregiving that require limitless patience and resourcefulness, but I have done a passable job at making sure to maintain a life of my own. This might sound like a selfish detour away from the matter at hand, but if you understand the long-term commitment of caring for an otherwise healthy person with Alzheimer's, and hear how some caregivers report "not having a life" or "losing themselves," never mind getting sick, depressed, or even suicidal, my attempts to keep track of myself start to look like an important adjunct to the work I do for my mom. And keeping track of myself—by taking walks in the forest, doing yoga, meeting with friends, or, sure, going to Egypt for three weeks—has required another kind of close examination of my relationship to truth.

In deciding whether or not to tell my mother about the often pleasant and rewarding life I try to lead, even as her life seems to be shrinking in on her, I apply the four-fold question: is it true, is it kind, is it necessary, does it do harm? Early on, when I saw my mother withdrawing from the world and consequently having fewer and fewer opportunities to go out and do things, I felt sheepish and guilty leaving her at home when I was going out to do something fun. If she asked, "What are you doing today?" I found it easier to say, "Oh, just some work I have to do" than "Meeting with a friend for a walk and some tea." Wasn't that the kinder path? Over time I have come to reevaluate this aspect of truth telling and have come to look at answering questions about my choices a little differently. Now I think about answering questions like "What are you doing today?" as an opportunity to exercise a truth-telling muscle that will serve both myself and my mother far longer than lies meant to protect her will. It doesn't really make sense to pretend to her—for her sake—that I don't have anything going on in my life apart from my work and spending time with her, so answering the question honestly has become my mental / emotional biceps curl. "I'm going to meet up with a friend." "I'm going to do yoga." "I'm going out to lunch." The truth telling muscle gets stronger; the sky doesn't fall; and I maintain my sense of self. Is it kind? I don't say it to rub salt in the wound. I say it to stay present to myself so that I'll continue to have a self that can care for my mother.

At support group one day a woman shared a similar method of getting out from under the guilt that telling the truth often provokes. She said that instead of feeling guilt for all the things she can still do in her life (take a walk on her own, go to a movie, get in her car and drive)—things unavailable to the one she cared for—she turns it around and expresses to herself that she feels regret at all they've lost. Regret seems to be an emotion we are better able to process, she said, and saying to herself, "I regret that this disease keeps you from doing what you'd otherwise want to do in life," allows her to get out from under the guilt she might feel about her own abilities and freedoms.

When I decided that that my husband, son, and I should take a three-week trip to Egypt, I based the decision on several factors, working hard to keep guilt at arm's length. First, I had told my son that if he stuck with Arabic language lessons for three years, we could go. He'd done that. Second, I knew that I'd never go to Egypt on my own or with my husband. It just wasn't our kind of trip. But with a kid interested in pyramids and mummies and all that, who still had a child's sense of wonder for the world, then yes, why not. Third, tempus fugit. None of us were getting younger, and, I figured, things would only get worse for my mom later on. If we were going to go, it should be sooner than later. My mom might have Alzheimer's, but I wasn't going to live forever, either.

If telling truths about the daily goings on in my life was like a healthy number of biceps curls, then telling her about this trip was like a dozen reps of one-armed pushups. It took focus, balance, and repetition. But anyway, there was no point in lying. We had our tickets and we were going. At that stage in the disease, just two years after diagnosis, she still insisted she was perfectly fine and I had not yet found a way to get her to see otherwise. If my daily presence in her life, her doctor's strong warnings, and her short stint in counseling couldn't stop her from drinking, denying how much she drank, and covering for all her losses, then I assumed only the long progression of the disease could. Meanwhile, I'd be gone for just three weeks, and then I'd resume my efforts to give care when I got back. Where she'd be then was hard to know given the uneven progression of the disease, but staying home was unlikely to stop it in its tracks.

What most research on Alzheimer's shows is a stair-step pattern of loss. Steep declines followed by plateaus that can last months or even a year. Then another decline, then another stage of relative stability. The grade and depth of these steps will vary depending on the person's general health and other factors, including: do they still live at home, with friends and family nearby, or have they just moved? If they've moved, do they understand where they are? Have they had time to adjust? Will they ever adjust?

Where the parent with Alzheimer's should live, and the elusive goal of stability that question raises, becomes a major focus for caregivers. Assisted living facilities—I use the term broadly to include everything from active senior retirement communities to just short of locked memory care units— promote the idea of "aging in place." The idea is that if we get our loved ones into a new setting early, they will have time to acclimate while they still have the cognitive skills to learn new routines, make friends, and take advantage of programs. This is a lovely idea in theory, and some active seniors I know are considering making this move: downsizing, getting away from large, demanding gardens, opting for a living situation that will free them up for travel and will provide a safety net that includes community, transportation, and meals. These are people who embrace the idea of letting go, and these are just the people many senior retirement homes would love to have—to make their places look vibrant and alive, not like warehouses for the decrepit.

The important distinction between those aging with health and those entering dementia is that the latter group, for the most part, does not want to admit that they are losing their capacity; "letting go" is the enemy, not a materially or spiritually liberating ideal. I had briefly considered trying to get my mom to move before we went to Egypt, thinking that she'd be safer, well looked after, and set up for the next stage of her life. The conversation my mother and I had around this topic, at least 500 times, went something like this:

"I'll probably need to move into one of those homes some day. It might not be too bad."

"Yes, it might be nice. You might like it."

"I remember when I visited Mary in that place where she lived. She went down for meals or could have them in her room. One woman had a cat. It was nice."

"Yes, and there'd be activities, and there'd always be people around you could talk to."

"But I'm not lonely here. I've never been outgoing. I am happy in this house."

"Well, sometimes you say you're lonely."

"That's true. But I don't think I need to go into a home yet. When it's time, I will. But I don't think I need to go yet. Do you?"

"How will you know when it's time?"

"Oh, if I don't lock the door at night, or if I leave the stove on. But I haven't done those things."

"Well, you have left the keys in the front door on a few occasions. I don't know if you've left the stove on. How would I know?"

"Well, I haven't. I'd know. I love this house. I hope I can stay here till I die."

Sometimes the loop left me dizzy from the speed at which we made the full round.

"I get lonely in this house all day."

"If you moved into a place, you'd have people to talk to and things to do."

"I don't really feel lonely. I've never been outgoing. I love this house. I hope I can stay here till I die."

I stopped viewing her opening lines about boredom or loneliness as my golden ticket into the next stage of caregiving—the getting your loved one into a safer environment stage—early in the process, and I abandoned it completely in the countdown to our trip. As surely as she began the conversation with a glimmer of possibility that she'd consider moving, she'd end the conversation with the reaffirmation that she wanted to die right where she was, at home, ideally in a Thelma & Louise-like pact with her dog.

Getting the dementia sufferer to move into some kind of facility—if that's the path you plan on taking—presents one of the biggest hurdles in caregiving, right up there with selling the car and taking over finances. Many have been very clever in how they've gotten their parent to move. One woman at group told her mother that she was going to stay in a fancy hotel, and "Look mom, free meals!" Some have misfortune work in their favor: a flooded basement, a leaky roof, usually the problem gets exaggerated. These emergencies and the cost to repair them, caregivers tell their parent, make it impossible for them to remain at home.

It would be easier if there were a logical and consistent order of events in caring for a person with Alzheimer's, that the stages of the disease came with a corresponding to-do list: confiscate car keys, take over finances, move the person out of her home, etc. And you might wish that the list could also describe the rise and run of the stair-step decline, laying out how, exactly, we get from here to there without tripping on an unseen ledge. But just as the order of events for young people moving toward family life has been thrown out the window—is it get a dog, buy a house, have a child, and then get married?, or have a child, get the dog, marry, then move back home?—so, too, with the checklist for Alzheimer's care. While most caregivers will hit every milestone listed here, very few do so in the same order.

Start making and attending medical/dental appointments
Ditto for pets
Manage medications
Oversee finances
Take the car
Manage transportation
Unplug the stove
Oversee nutrition
Hire other caregivers to help out
Move the person; repeat as necessary
Get Power of Attorney (POA) for Healthcare
Update the will, if necessary
Look at all banking and insurance issues
Sell the house
Select a facility; possibly repeat
Oversee staff at the facility; repeat
Dismantle a life

Each of these has its own subset of activities and anxieties and can, on its own, take years to accomplish. Each adds to the necessary calculation of rise and run. Better medication management and improved nutrition might extend a plateau by a year; taking the car away might result in a precipitous decline. If you are able to move your loved one early, some of the steps will be combined. But that doesn't mean you are, in any way, off the hook.

One of my greatest eye-opening moments at support group came when I realized that caregivers still had to give care when their loved one moved into a facility, whether just mildly assisted or fully locked. Experienced caregivers will scoff at my ignorance, but there it is. I assumed, at some early, naïve stage of the journey, that my caregiving work required me to see my mother to the entrance of the tunnel to Shangri-La, and that after that I could, as one assisted living sales manager assured me, "just come visit your mom and not worry."

Caregivers, both amateur and professional, have different levels of receptivity to the language and gestures of people with dementia. Some take a more psychoanalytic approach and might suggest that my mother's opening gambits about moving "into a home," as she always put it, were tantamount to waiving the white flag of surrender. That secretly she really did want to move, that she was frightened by living alone, that she wanted more company and support, but that she was trapped by her conditioned habit of rejecting offers of help. These are the professionals who've told me that when my mother repeatedly said, "You can just drop me off; I don't want to be any trouble," when the plan was to spend more time together, what she really was telling me was, "I'm tired and I want to go home." Is that what she meant? It's hard to know. Her life was, and is, far from an open book.

Around the topic of moving, however, I think I read her clearly. When we visited several places in town—once on St.

Patrick's Day, where, I kid you not, a bagpipe player was stationed in the 20ft x 40ft dining area, blasting residents and guests with holiday cheer—my mom could barely sustain her polite veneer. Even in rooms that had a view of Mt. Baker, or a pleasant back deck, or a light, open layout, she wore the expression of someone who'd just smelled a corpse.

What she did say, when she would comment at all, was that she didn't want a room where she'd have to see the kitchen all day. Some of the larger rooms we looked at did indeed have small kitchen areas—a sink, a refrigerator, a stove top or hot plate, a microwave, a countertop—but most had just a few tiny appliances tucked into a small corner: maybe a quarter-sized sink and a mini-fridge topped by a tiny microwave. I told my mom that we could easily put up a screen to separate the living area from the kitchen, that with her tables and plants and art, the straight on view of those appliances could easily be eliminated. But no. Every room we looked at had some kind of kitchen in the entry way, and there was no way around it: If your intention was to stand in the open, unfurnished living room and stare at the kitchen, you could. On these visits she never came right out and said, "I refuse to move," but she didn't have to; she could simply repeat her new mantra. I got flippant. "You wouldn't see it from the shower," I'd quip, or, "You could just avert your eyes."

Leaving these places, my mom shrunk into herself in the passenger seat, keeping her jaw set, her eyes straight ahead, her lips drawn into a thin, lifeless line. Sometimes she'd make a shuddering movement, like a dog shaking off water. At those times I thought I could understand her pretty clearly, and it was in those moments that I needed acting school more than ever. I could never quite rally myself to feign the necessary enthusiasm to say, "That place was fabulous, wasn't it? I think you'd be so happy there!" Even if I didn't have her glacial response to overcome, which would be hard enough, I had my own cold reaction to what we'd seen. The managers never seemed to quite get my mom's personality; the hallways were so long that I could see my mother getting lost on her way to meals; the other residents were all on walkers, and I could imagine my mother asking them, in that slightly passive-aggressive way she sometimes affected, "Do you want to go for a walk?"

It's not that I can't lie, or won't. I remember Annie's lie of compassion. It's just that some lies are harder to carry off. How could I lie to myself that I thought any of these places would work out, then lie to my mom and say that I thought it would be perfect, and also lie to the facility about what I believed would happen if she moved in, which was, quite simply, that she'd walk out the front door and head home? I so preferred to just say what I felt. And what I felt, and eventually said to my mother during those conversational loop de loops about moving, was my version of an ultimatum: "Okay, if you don't want to move that's fine, but you're going to have to let people come in and help you at home." That would also evoke the corpse-sniffing face of doom, plus a silent shudder, but I couldn't help myself and sugar coating it just wasn't in me.

The same was true of Egypt. I didn't lie about the fact that we were going away. When my mom could remember to ask me about the trip, when it was still ahead of us, I told the truth. No, thank you, it's a kind offer, but we didn't want her to watch the dogs. Thanks anyway. I said we'd be gone three weeks, that we'd made some arrangements for her to get some help with pills and such, that if she needed anything, she could call Paul's sister. And that was that until my resolve was shaken on the morning before our departure, when I went over to get her for our usual walk and saw that all the blinds were still drawn at 10 a.m. and that there was an open beer on her living room table. I noticed that her speech seemed a little slurred. I did a quick check for evidence of a possible stroke, and finding that her smile was symmetrical enough and she could raise her arms evenly, I deduced that she'd simply hit the beer early, and on an empty stomach, possibly thinking that it was already evening in the darkened room. Hard truths of a sad situation, but I had to ask myself if my not going to Egypt would stop her from drinking. No. It hadn't yet. Shaken but not deterred, I carried on. Sometimes I couldn't help feel selfish and cruel that we were going away, but we were, and lying didn't seem like it would help.

The reason I even tell the Egypt story is that it worked. We got away, and my mom did just fine. We had a strange, educational, bizarre, beautiful, once-in-a-lifetime adventure. We were home exactly 27 days before the uprising began that resulted in the revolution that turned everything on its head, but while we were there, we would never have guessed that anything was about to break through the thick fog of resignation and suspicion that most of the friendly people we met there seemed to accept as a natural way of being. We were completely out of our element, immersed in a land and culture as far away from our insular, gray Bellingham lives as possible, and miracle of miracles, my mom did perfectly fine in our absence.

One sweet woman at support group said that she never wanted to be more than five hours away from her mother. Five hours by car, a shorter time if she could manage a flight. Her mother was at a later stage of the disease than my mom, but still, I couldn't believe it. Or maybe her dedication made me feel guilty. How could she live with that short of a tether? I knew I would show up for my mother when I had to, and I'd continue to manage all the care I could, but I also wanted to reserve the right to be more than five hours away. I wanted a tether that would reach as far as Lake Nassar, where we'd taken a four-day cruise and disembarked on desert shores to see remote temples, some of which had been painstakingly moved and reassembled when the Aswan dam stopped the flow of the Nile and flooded the valley. Like the ruins, I wanted to stay above water as long as possible. Giving myself space and distance was one way I thought I could do it.

5. TAKING CARE

My mother went back to school in her early 40s to get a nursing degree. Married a year or two out of high school, she hadn't gone to college and had been a stay-at-home mom since she was about 24. She got a 4.0 while raising three rebellious teenagers and unwittingly approaching the end of her 25-year marriage to my dad. She could not look happier or more nurse-like in the photo taken at her graduation, where she walks down the aisle wearing the standard issue white nurse's dress and clip-on cap that was part of the uniform 35 years ago. Carrying a candle and smiling proudly, she appears to have no idea what lay just ahead.

After the divorce, she got a job at a hospital across town and was a kind and effective giver of care, but she didn't love the work. Ironically, the same nursing shortage that initially encouraged her to get the degree made the job nearly impossible with all its thankless demands on the understaffed crew. Working the afternoon shift didn't suit her, and it probably wasn't very good for me, either, leaving me, then a high school senior, unsupervised from the time school let out till about 11 p.m. We were, in our own ways, adrift and slightly desperate, but holding on.

She kept that job through the first year of my college life, and then she'd had enough. She invested some of her divorce settlement into a share of Kentucky Fried Chicken restaurants a friend of a friend was buying in Northern California. And then, to everyone's surprise, she asked if she could work there, too. The investment seemed sketchy at first but paid off in the end; the job seemed comical, and was. But it gave her a ticket out of Phoenix and into a new life in South Lake Tahoe that included a rise through the ranks of the 20-something employees to become a manager of her own KFC in Mammoth Lakes; respectful friendships with the illegal workers from Mexico and El Salvador who helped her succeed; and an awkward proposal of marriage from one 20-year-old more desperate than others for his green card. She was a good friend to that prematurely stooped, pencil-thin young man with the sorrowful face, even giving him a place to live when he was short of rent. But she drew the line at marrying him.

The two years she spent on this detour from her real life, as she put it later, didn't save her from the grief she experienced at being left by my dad, but it did give her plenty of distraction. "Then one day," she'd say about this time, "I decided to go back to my regular life." She stayed in California but moved south, near San Luis Obispo, and eventually found a job working in the county mental health clinic. More service work, this time giving practical guidance to those with serious, lifelong needs. She loved it. With her nursing degree she could dispense meds, which is what qualified her for the job, and after that she blossomed into a full-time mental health case worker. Early on she ran a program that helped teach life skills—including teaching clients how to shop for groceries, cook meals, and possibly live on their own. She transported clients around town like a carpooling mom, getting kids here and there, telling them to quiet down if it got too noisy, making jokes, keeping an eye on the rear view mirror. She was comfortable with them and could be herself—caring, funny, and no-nonsense when she needed to be.

One of her favorite stories from that era, one she remembered through the early stages of Alzheimer's when many other things had been forgotten or confused—like whether or not she eloped, whether or not her father was still alive—is one of our favorites, too, the one with "penis" in its punch line. It happened when she took some of her mental health clients to a large Safeway market in downtown San Luis Obispo. The store had a bunch of checkout aisles that on this particular day had lines several shoppers deep, herself and several of her clients among them. She was standing there waiting her turn, probably helping her clients with a few pointers about patience and social decorum, when one of them said in a voice loud enough for everyone to hear, "Pat, does that man have his penis on my head?" My mom's face lights up when she gets to this point in the story, and she gestures with both hands, like a conductor quieting the strings, to show the magnitude of the question's effect. "Everyone just stopped what they were doing and looked over at us. And I just said, 'No Sean, that man's penis is not on your head.' And he said, 'Oh, Okay.'" She had grown inured to strangers' looks of fear and disapproval. Her clients must have trusted her implicitly. She knew how to help them. She knew, deeply, that they were doing the best they could with what they had.

Only ten years elapsed between the time my mother gave this kind of care to others and started to need it for herself. But even during those ten years, the years of slow, nearly imperceptible decline, she gave care as a volunteer in various capacities and as a loving grandma. And, in her way, she still gives care: by cooing at babies, patting people's shoulders, and offering help that she can't possibly deliver. A recent statistic from the Alzheimer's Society reports that someone receives an Alzheimer's diagnosis every 67 seconds—and that's still only about half of the people who actually have it. How many of the millions now needing care were the ones we once counted on to deliver it?

In *Being Mortal*, Atul Gawande shares the sobering news that fewer doctors are choosing to go into geriatric medicine even though the demand for geriatricians is on the rise. He cites the "unsexy" nature of the specialty—the time it takes to get through an appointment; dealing with the garden variety ailments of old age on top of the unavoidable one, mortality; meeting and talking to sometimes uncomprehending and often non-compliant patients. All that plus lower salaries and poor Medicare reimbursement rates, and you can hardly blame these young people who've just spent 80 thousand dollars on their education and want to feel like they're making a positive change in the world. Gawande points out that geriatricians actually do, however, make huge improvements in the lives of those they treat—that if they could package as a device what they do for patients through their routine care, extending the years our older generation can live independently and without more costly interventions, "we'd be clamoring for it." It's not anything fancy like a device, though:

> Instead, it was just geriatrics. The geriatric teams weren't doing lung biopsies or back surgery. . . What they did was to simplify medications. They saw that arthritis was controlled. They made sure toenails were trimmed and meals were square. They looked for worrisome signs of isolation and had a social worker check that the patient's home was safe.

This was the kind of simplified, human care my mother delivered to the mentally ill clients she worked with in the last five years of her working life, before she retired to move here, and fittingly, it's the kind of care she receives from her geriatric nursing specialist. For this, we are fortunate.

You don't have to look hard to see the downside of geriatric medicine, however, if dealing with old people's issues is not your thing. Unsexy is putting it mildly. At my mother's first office visit with her care provider, Erica, it occurred to me to ask my mother when she'd last seen a gynecologist. It seemed that it had been years, but before you start making and attending appointments with your parent, how would you know? I also had a niggling memory of something to do with uterine prolapse. Hadn't she been seen for that a while back, and wasn't she doing something about it? When it occurred to me to ask my mother about her gynecological health, it had been more than a year, I figured out later, since she'd thought anything about her uterine prolapse or the pessary her gynecologist had given her to alleviate her symptoms. Such is the sad and perplexing disconnect an Alzheimer's sufferer has with his or her body. Sense of smell is lost early in the process, so that's one more source of useful information that disappears. I broke the news to Erica with as much dignity as I could manage, on my mom's behalf, not concealing my sympathy for what Erica was going to have to do. Sure enough, the long-forgotten pessary was still in there. Kind, common-sense care: Erica let out a loud hoot when she extracted it and got it into the trash.

When you deal with people's illness, suffering, and loss, you take on the good, the bad, and the ugly. Fewer new doctors want the ugly, perhaps, but maybe it's only because they haven't learned to appreciate the profound good that comes from it that reaches beyond the patient to the caregivers and the communities that support them.

In attending to any patient, doctors and nurses walk the line of needing to address the person being treated and having to make sure the ones overseeing the care are on board. Pediatricians treat the child but speak to the parents. General practitioners treat the patient and speak to the patient. Geriatric specialists have to feel it out, case by case. They are treating and speaking to the patient in front of them, but if that patient suffers dementia, then communicating with the support team is equally important. In the best case scenario, everyone's needs get met.

But what about dealing with specialists? Specialists, and all those practitioners who don't have senior citizens as their primary demographic, can be, in my experience, a bit clueless when it comes to treating patients with Alzheimer's. While the geriatrician has notes to refer to and can look to the adult child or caregiver for more information, the specialists my mom has seen have, at various stages on this path, been obstinately committed to talking directly to my mother about things she was ill equipped to discuss or understand. Examples abound.

When my mother had a small "stage zero" melanoma, and surgery was recommended to remove it, I was shocked to hear on the day of her surgery and for the very first time a reminder that she'd need a 24-hour in-home observation period afterward. Someone must have called her in the lead up to the surgery date and given her this information, but none of it ever got to me. Did they think she could remember the call five minutes after it ended, arrange care on her own, or convey a somewhat complex message to me? Perhaps I should have anticipated it, just like you'd anticipate staying in the hospital with a friend or family member, if possible, to make sure they got the care they needed. But having been mostly healthy and out of hospitals and surgery suites, I just didn't know, and no one had thought it necessary to tell me.

If the surgeon had treated my mother like a pediatric case with me standing in as the parent, I'm sure I would have received better, clearer, more helpful information about her follow-up care. Instead, on the day of her surgery I heard, for the first time, what they were going to do, how long it would take, and what she was supposed to do afterward to care for her incision. No doctor would tell a 9-year old to change her own bandages and watch for infection, but some, apparently, have no hesitation asking a person with Alzheimer's to take on that level of self-care.

If this only happened once, I might chalk it up to the inexperience of that doctor, though I'm sure his specialty—

removing melanomas—puts him in the company of the elderly more often than not. But over and over I find myself having to tell medical professionals that the instructions or recommendations they're giving need to be simplified, redirected, or eliminated altogether. Is their yearning to help the patient in front of them so strong that they can't see the limited good of that one-to-one communication? Have the laws surrounding privacy and confidentiality shackled them into patterns of behavior that simply don't work? Or is this just uncharted territory that is only getting mapped now, by my mom's generation and the adult children trying to find their way?

Take the time my mom's dentist prescribed a night guard. Seriously? Before I had the confidence to step in and refuse what would later become a category of care I could only call "impossible to comply with," I went along with this recommendation, setting up appointment times and paying the bills. At some future appointment the dentist checked in about the night guard only to be met with that blank acknowledgement my mom gave when she didn't have a clue. "Oh, it's fine," or "Uh huh." The night guard was nowhere to be found, but even if I set it on her bed side table every night and took possession of it every morning, who could say if she'd actually wear it?

It's vexing that medical professionals don't seem to understand the chasm between their well meaning instructions and the patient's ability to comply. Nor do many of these care providers see how they have to widen the circle of care beyond the client they're treating. It's irritating, but you have to get past that if you want to keep your sanity. As one wise man at support group observed, as a caregiver you have to establish relationships with everyone in the circle of care. You learn quickly that you have to be sure that the office has your phone number as the primary contact and that you have to serve two functions in any appointment. You have to ask questions your loved one might ask if she could remember to ask them, and you have to ask questions whose answers you need. You have to show up, follow up, and be persistent. But even the best laid plans go south.

Take the pharmacy, for example. The pharmacy I contacted and made arrangements with to get a monthly mediset established, the same one that fills my mother's Alzheimer's prescription every month (a clue to her condition?!), repeatedly forgot/misread/lost notes in my mom's chart that instructed them to call me instead of my mother. For at least a year I'd encounter head-scratching mysteries including a month's worth of meds that got delivered to my mother's house and disappeared after she "put them away," unanswered messages about prescription refills, and pills being divided up into their a.m. and p.m. slots differently, for no apparent reason.

Nothing is simple. At a veterinary appointment the vet came back with the results of my mom's dog's blood work and told my mom the sad news: Doozy was suffering worsening kidney function, infection, probable pain. To treat it, the dog would need two pills and two different eye drops delivered three times a day. My mom was not near ready to let the dog go, so of course she agreed to treat her with pills and whatever else as long as she could. Or, as long as "we" could. But three times a day? Consider the logistics: a caregiver would have to be hired to get to my mom's house at some midday time when I was at work. But even my mom wasn't home every midday, so that new caregiver would have to be vetted, given a key, and shown how to give a very resistant, fragile dog two pills and eye drops. The pills would have to be divided up and distributed to everyone administering them (because if we left the bottle at my mom's house, they'd be "put away" and disappear), and everyone on the job would have to be shown how to watch Doozy for a while to see that she didn't stash the pills in her cheek then spit them up later, as she was known to do.

I knew all this; how did the vet not foresee similar challenges? Did the vet choose to ignore my mother's obvious dementia and all her repetitions of the same questions, her anxiety, her simple, uncomprehending answers? Did she not see in the chart that I'd called and told the office that my mom had Alzheimer's and that I was the contact person? Or did she see it but decide that it was still her professional obligation to talk to my mom and not to me? Did she think it would help preserve my mother's dignity and autonomy? But what about the dog?

Caregivers have to decide when to intervene, even when it feels like challenging authority in areas where they have zero expertise. Not wanting to sound heartless, not wanting to discount my mom's devotion to her dog, I said, "It's not possible to give pills and eye drops three times a day. Don't you have something that can be administered just once?" The answer was no, so we compromised on a protocol that could be given in two doses. A small victory in an obscure battle in the ongoing war. But I'd take it.

Then there are all the service professions one has to deal with as a caregiver that have nothing to do with health or medical services, like home repair folks, lawn service people, bankers, and grocery store clerks. After hearing my mom say that she better get up on the roof and clean out her gutters, I took her ladder away and then contacted a roof and gutter cleaning company to get a bid on the job. I sent an email and left a phone message explaining the situation: the job was at my mom's house, but I would be the contact person at a different phone number and address. A couple weeks later I got word from one of my mom's visitors that someone had been over there to look at the roof, so presumably delivered the bid, but not to me, and I never heard another word from them. Instead of calling and leaving a third message about our situation—one that clearly can't be all that unique—I decided to try again with a different company and found one that got it right the first time.

As a bath remodeling specialist I met with to get a bid on removing my mom's bathtub unit and replacing it with a walk-in shower told me, boomers are aging. This is big business. So maybe some businesses will get this new reality and thrive while others will stick with the status quo and fail. Maybe businesses will get savvy and add some shorthand to their company mission statements, something straightforward like "dementia specialists," or something more subtle, like "let us help."

But then there's the flip side. For every business that's slow to catch on to the special needs of a client with dementia and the care team that's acting on his or her behalf, there are those unscrupulous ones eager to cash in on forgetfulness. Rarely does a support group wrap up without at least one story about a parent subscribing to every magazine offer that comes in the mail or sending checks to all the charities that call. It doesn't take much for many of our parents—lonely, still wanting to make decisions on their own, confused about what they've already signed up for and who they've already paid—to fall victim to various kinds of hucksters. If my mom were not so naturally cheap, these solicitations would be a constant worry.

Sometimes it's hard to see how these holes in the social fabric can ever be mended. Japan has taken a positive approach to the problem of an aging and increasingly Alzheimer's-ridden population, as has at least one "dementia-friendly" community in Minnesota. Instead of crafting legislation to tell children what they have to do for their parents, as China has tried through its "filial piety laws," Japan has trained 5.4 million volunteers to help identify wanderers and offer respite care to burned-out caregivers in order to keep the elderly from being left on *obasuteyama*, or "granny-dump mountain." In this load-sharing scheme described in a 2015 *Economist* magazine article, Japanese retailers "train staff to help shoppers who have become confused, and to deal sympathetically with elderly customers who go off with items they have forgotten to pay for, or try to pay for twice." In Paynesville, Minnesota, a training program instructs merchants and service workers to speak directly and clearly to customers with dementia, and to never argue. Just like in Japan, the goal is to keep people out of all our myriad forms of granny-dump mountain by helping them feel included, supported, and engaged in the community.

Education campaigns? Legislation? Maybe, sadly, the sheer number of people developing some form of dementia in the near future will trigger inventive and necessary solutions. I envision more services that will become available—something like national "do not call" registries, only more sweeping and protective—and more service agencies that will pop up to support families trying to give care. Of course, my mother is blessedly unaware of the complications that arise from her condition. She still doesn't think she has a condition. If anyone suggested to her that care was needed, it's clear which side of the giving she'd be on. She'd pat the shoulder of the caregiver and ask how she could help.

6. BOUNDARIES

The metaphorical statement "I draw a line in the sand" never made a lot of sense to me. You draw a line and you don't go past it, or if you do, you can't go back. But isn't the very nature of sand that it is malleable and impermanent? Who hasn't made a sand castle and a moat, a deeper kind of "line" in the sand, only to see it dissolve in an unexpected wave and be re-absorbed into the beach? Those are the kinds of lines in the sand I have drawn through the early years of caregiving, and may still draw to preserve my sanity. I draw one and stick to it, but then a wave comes and I start all over again.

At the earliest stages of the Alzheimer's journey, my line was about friendship and company. I told myself that I wouldn't feel responsible or guilty for my mom not having any more friends; I wouldn't step up to try to be her all and every-thing. Much later in the journey, as her ability to cook for her-self diminished, she refused the help of caregivers when it came to cooking meals. She'd pull them out of her kitchen by the elbow, scoffing at their concerns that she needed some dinner, insisting she'd make something later. I drew a line at that point, thinking, "Fine. If she won't accept their help she can eat whatever she can put together on her own. I'm not cooking for her!" Both lines were obliterated by the rising tide of the illness. It's not so much that I refused to ultimately cross them or that I crossed and could never go back. It's more that the sand shifted entirely, and as my mom changed, I changed, too.

That is not to say, however, that caregivers shouldn't create boundaries. Like lines in the sand, they may shift and change, but without them, heading into the ill-defined stage of life called "caring for a parent with dementia" is like walking into the desert without sunglasses. They're not all you'll need on the journey, but they help you relax and see a little more clearly.

We might think that boundaries are only necessary in unhealthy personal or workplace situations, or that boundaries only need erecting when one party means to take advantage of another. Depending very much on the way you grew up, your place in your family, and the general health or dysfunction of that unit, you may look at boundaries as strange and unnecessary obstacles to a closeness you have had, or want to have, with your parent. Or, like me, you take comfort in this idea of a fence, a border, possibly a lovely yew hedge, separating you from all that lies just beyond your comfort zone. Pema Chodron, my favorite teacher on all things related to maintaining one's sanity, guides me in my thinking. Responding to a woman who wanted to know how she could visit her dysfunctional family at holiday times while maintaining her integrity and not getting run over or dragged back into old patterns of destructive behavior, Chodron answered, "The Buddha would have loved boundaries." If the Buddha would have loved this 20th century idea that we need to create and maintain healthy physical, mental, emotional, and spiritual boundaries between ourselves and the people who, intentionally or without meaning to, pull us off course, then so should we.

Many caregivers who try to establish healthy boundaries sabotage their own efforts by simultaneously blaming themselves for being selfish. They imagine that other caregivers are more giving, more patient, more selfless in their time and dedication. And maybe some are. But should 'selflessness' really be the goal? Literally without a self? My desire for boundaries had to do with preserving energy for the things I wanted to do in my life apart from my relationship with my mother: work, be in a marriage, raise a child, cultivate friendships, care for pets, maintain a house, develop talents that take time and practice. It also came, I'm sure, from the part of my mother's sorrow that had become mine. My father left my mother when I was 17 and the last child living at home, so I was the main witness to her grief. After graduating from high school, I came home from college to spend weekends with her in that sadly empty house. When she needed to get out of Phoenix to escape her painful memories, I was the one who drove her to North Lake Tahoe and tried to offer comfort as she cried. And I spent parts of my summers with her after she moved, watching her try to navigate through loneliness into a new life. And then I saw her begin to heal, and I hoped that she could recover fully—not just from the divorce, but from childhood, too, from being that "orphan girl" for so long—and become whole.

A lot of the lines we draw as caregivers seem to have nothing to do with us. They aren't boundaries to protect personal space; they are the dividing lines between what's safe and unsafe, what's tolerable and intolerable. They seem obvious and factual, but it doesn't always work out that way. You might say to yourself, "Okay, if she leaves her stove on, we'll have to remove it." But then you notice that maybe you've left the stove on once or twice. Are you going to remove yours, too? You second guess yourself. Well-meaning friends and onlookers want to cut the dementia sufferer the most slack, agreeing that they, too, are always looking for their keys, losing their wallet, forgetting to balance the checkbook. Even the most conscientious caregivers will rationalize a lot of aberrant behavior, chalking it up to a bad day, or a new routine, or, sympathetically, they'll see it as a natural enough response to a devastating disease.

With the support of my mom's geriatrician I drew lines in the sand about drinking that kept getting washed away in my own muddle over how to keep an accurate count. Four bottles in the fridge plus another store receipt that showed a 12-pack minus ten bottles in the trash can . . . where were the other six?! Other lines, like the one I drew around her practice of lighting long, tapered candles every night and dimming the lights in her living room while she drank, stayed pretty firmly intact. (Solution: steal all the candles!)

About seven months after my mom's official diagnosis of Alzheimer's, almost five years from when she first complained that her GP wasn't taking her complaints about memory loss seriously, her geriatrician told her that she shouldn't be driving any more. She took my mom's memory loss seriously and laid it on the line. She told my mom no more drinking, no more driving. My mom left that appointment weeping, but in agreement. I thought, "Really? That's all it takes? Why didn't I try that?" She told the doctor: I can stop. I can quit. I will quit drinking today.

Those who've been spending their time at Al-Anon meetings instead of Alzheimer's support groups might guess that it wasn't so simple. Even as I left that appointment with my mom, gratified and relieved that Erica had been so firm and had gotten my mom to agree to these new terms, I felt suspicious. And I felt a bit framed, too. Now I not only had to monitor my mom to see that she complied with her own agreement—no drinking and no driving—but I had to be the one to enforce the rules if she tried to skirt back across the lines she'd crossed. It was one thing to theorize that the time had come for her to stop driving; it was another thing to actually enforce it.

Hearing stories from fellow caregivers about how they get their loved one to stop driving is like watching a new adaptation of a story you already know. How will it go this time, you wonder, settling in for the new twist on the old tale. Will there be zombies? Every time a new person comes to a support group still on the car side of that particular line in the sand, we await their approach to the crisis eager to hear how it unfolds.

Our saga played out over a dramatic few months during which time my mother must have been leaving something on when she parked the car because the battery in that otherwise unstoppable old Volvo kept dying. Some mechanically minded caregivers actually unplug the battery to make sure the car won't start, but that wouldn't have worked with my mom because she still knew how to use a phone. She just called her mechanic and had someone come out to fix it. After two of these incidents I called the mechanic myself and asked him to stall her the next time she called and to call me and let me know. He said he'd try, but I could tell he wouldn't try very hard. He had a business to run, he probably didn't have a mother with dementia, and he clearly didn't want to work on his creative lying skills. So when the car died again, he fixed it.

Another appointment with the geriatrician, another agreement about driving, this time in writing. I love these. We've written "contracts" a few times along this journey, and of these I can only say, nice try. In the lingo of Alzheimer's care, a contract that attempts to prevent future behavior represents a "mismatch" between a caregiver's expectations and a dementia sufferer's comprehension. But in our defense, my mother presented well, and for brief moments she seemed to understand that driving was a dangerous risk to herself and others. She agreed to sell the car, and then she didn't. She'd express relief that I was going to take care of it for her, even agreeing that "it was time," and then she'd express outrage that I was stealing her car.

One time when we'd been out in her car, I asked if I could drop her off at her house and drive myself home so that I could be there in time to meet a friend who was coming over.

Usually pretty agreeable, she said no. She wanted to go to the store. For what? I asked, knowing for what. We wrangled over the topic of beer for a few minutes, but the clock was ticking and I needed to get home. I also knew, however, that if I had her drop me off at my house, she'd go directly to the store to buy beer. I put on a loving, easy breezy act to cut through the tension, barreled forward with my plan, and left my mother standing in her driveway, still fuming that she wanted to go to the store. I said I'd be back later, hoping time would lessen her anger, and drove home. But halfway there I glanced down and noticed that my mom had left her purse in the car. So now I had taken the car AND her purse, a point she was still cognizant enough to realize. By the time I got home she had already called and left an angry message, so I called back to explain that I had only meant to borrow her car, not take her purse. Easy breezy wasn't cutting it. Ever the walker, and fast when she wanted to be, she marched the half mile over to my house to reclaim her belongings.

It wasn't pretty. My son loitered just inside, my husband came home in the middle of it, and my friend showed up right then, too. Susan pulled into the driveway right behind my mom's car, and my mother interpreted this as an orchestrated plot to box in her car and trap her. Have I mentioned the barking dogs? Susan had brought her noisy beagle, Maggie, and Maggie and my two dogs had commenced their loud and lengthy greeting. Unable to keep up any semblance of good cheer, I handed over the keys and purse and that was that. There was really nothing else to say. Or there was, but I didn't have my wits to say it.

She was ready to give up driving, and then she wasn't. Flip flop, back and forth, over and over. Somewhere in there, when she was most agreeable to the idea, I got her to sign the title. Soon after that she was calling to say she would call the police if I didn't bring her car back. When the day of the sale actually came, thank god the people were decisive and had cash in hand. We'd taken the car with my mother's blessing that morning, but as we spoke with the potential buyers, I kept glancing down the street expecting to see her marching our way, face set, eyes steely. I wondered if they'd still buy the car if my mom showed up and started calling me a thief. Somehow we avoided that scene.

It is the paradox of caregiving that even when you are carrying out a doctor's orders, following the sound advice of others who've gone before you, and trusting and acting on your own strong intuition, you can give excellent care and still feel like a heartless criminal.

Eliminating driving was a huge relief, no question. But as anyone who has sold, disabled, or "lost the keys" to their parent's car will know, that's just the beginning of a new stage of loss rather than the end of losing. Unless your loved one is at an assisted residence of some kind where transportation is part of the service—and your loved one is confident and capable enough to use it—you will take on your new role as taxi driver and errand runner. But however attentive you are in that new capacity, it cannot make up for the loss of freedom driving represents. Even now, when my mom exclaims that she could never find her way home from the park we just visited or the restaurant we just ate at, she'll still say, "I wish I could just get in the car and drive somewhere." On that point she is totally in agreement with my teenage son.

For the first little while after we sold my mom's car, we talked happily about all the money she was saving. No more car insurance, no maintenance costs, no gas, no taxes, no more quarters into the downtown parking meters. Hurray! With all that she was saving, I cajoled, she could take a taxi anywhere she wanted to go. Just call and go! (Never mind that she didn't have a cell phone, and even if she did, wouldn't know how to use it to call for a ride home. But I was being enthusiastic!) Or she could call me. And even without having to call—here I worked hard to sound upbeat and persuasive, knowing that if I went shopping with her it would mean regular confrontations about her consumption of beer—we would go to the store as often as she wanted.

And want she did, for a remarkably long time, but not with me. For two and a half years, from the time we got rid of the car in February, 2011, to my next major incursion into her freedom in August, 2013, she must have gone to the store about five or six times a week. Mostly she went on her own; sometimes she took Doozy. As I have already explained, my mom was in excellent physical health and an avid walker, so she'd walk to the store pulling her shopping cart with one hand and dragging the dog by its leash with the other. Almost daily.

The only things as regular in her life as her trips to the store were her anxious calls, asking us if we had her purse. Apart from that one time I'd accidentally driven away with it, the answer was no, followed quickly by our routine questions back to her: did you check the closet? Did you look upstairs? Sometimes we could help talk her out of her agitation by saying that her purse would show up, as it always did, or trying other means of distraction. We promised that we would watch her banking and credit card transactions online so that—in the off chance she did leave her purse somewhere—we'd know right away and would be able to cancel the card and put a hold on her checking account. Usually Paul or I ended up going over there to help her search. My lucky spots included the upstairs linen closet, under her bed, or somewhere in her clothes closet (I had to pat every item of clothing to find the purse tucked inside a shirt or sweater). Sometimes I'd find it on the hook in the pantry where it was supposed to be. Sometimes by the time I got over there to help her look she'd have already found it and forgotten the whole episode. She'd greet me at the door with a welcoming smile, thank me for coming, and have no idea that I was there because she'd just summoned me in a panic.

On many of these occasions—before calling us to ask if we'd seen her purse—my mother would have already called the bank or the credit card company. During that time I learned something new and disturbing about one arm of our financial system. You can be a 75-year-old woman with sufficient cognizance to walk a mile to the store to buy beer every other day and be simultaneously impaired enough to then call the credit card company to report that your purse had been stolen and get all those completely valid purchases wiped off your account. Do criminals know how easy this is? I had no idea! The first time this happened I called the credit card company to say, "Uh, no, actually my mother DID buy all that stuff; she just doesn't remember," but they wouldn't take my word for it. My Alzheimer's-afflicted mother could deny having purchased a bunch of beer, but I, her truth-honoring, caregiving daughter and Power of Attorney, could not get the charges reinstated because I wasn't a co-signer on her credit card account.

She denied making the purchases, she cancelled checks, she closed out whole accounts. Goodbye autopay! Every time she changed cards or stopped checks there'd be a short period of stamping out fires, clearing the smoke, seeing what remained standing. The routine of losing the purse became as predictable as it was tedious as it was heartbreaking. I'd see her purse hanging on its hook in the pantry knowing, sadly, that it was only a short time before the cycle would begin again. I tried not to think about all the hours she must have spent rummaging through drawers and closets and cupboards, angry at herself for what she could not control, then taking the few actions she still could: calling the bank, reporting the loss, starting over. Again and again and again.

But there was another aspect to this cycle that didn't elicit much sympathy in me. The part of me that saw "alcoholism" instead of "Alzheimer's" in her behavior had a hard time with her harrumphing indignation when she got her monthly statements and flatly denied that she could have spent that much money or gone to the store that often. And actually, it was never that much money. My mother has always been a cheapskate, so I could count my blessings where I found them. Though a massive Fred Meyer was one of the four stores on her circuit, she never went crazy on expensive purchases. Jewelry, electronics, clothes, furniture . . . those just weren't her thing. The frequency of her trips was something she also routinely denied. The credit card statements showed purchases from grocery stores made every other day, or sometimes three or four days in a row. I was used to her arguing with me over the always confounding tally of beer bottles, but now she was arguing with the credit card company about how often she went to the store to buy them.

At one of the many caregiver conferences I've attended over the years, Dr. Richard Powers spoke on the topic of "The Other Dementias." In making a point about how important early diagnosis is for ruling out other complicating or possibly reversible conditions, he got to the topic of alcohol-related dementia. That made my ears perk up. I had heard about Korsakoff Syndrome but had ruled this out as a possibility for my mother because her lab work never showed a thiamine (B-1) deficiency, nor had I ever seen or heard about her having an episode of Wernicke encephalopathy, also caused by severe lack of thiamine, which could be observed as very visible confusion, staggering and stumbling, lack of coordination, and abnormal involuntary eye movements. Powers said that even apart from these diagnosable conditions, there were other noticeable effects of alcohol on the brain, such as severe shrinkage of the lobes. Comfortingly, he said this level of damage would not be caused by a glass of wine or two at your child's wedding, but drink hard for ten or fifteen years, even if you stop in your early 50s, and yes, you might expect some irreversible damage.

His talk brought up a lot of the questions I thought I'd moved past or despaired of ever answering. How long had my mom been drinking so much? Did she have a period of drinking after her divorce that Powers would define as "hard"? Was it possible that she didn't have Alzheimer's but alcohol-related dementia? And painfully, had she brought it upon herself? Was that even a fair question? Do alcoholics bring it upon themselves? That was clearly a wrong way to think about it, but adult children caring for parents with Alzheimer's have been known to grasp at pretty flimsy straws when looking for reasons and explanations. If only we could blame it on canned tuna, a shortage of blueberries, or not doing enough crossword puzzles!

For me, this difficult issue of my mother's drinking kept coming back to other hard questions: What could I realistically do to help a person who was so independent, stubborn, physically fit, addicted, in denial, and past the point of benefiting from psychoanalytical approaches? How could I, or anyone, make inroads into her deeply rooted problems when the neuronal pathways that might get us there were blocked and tangled?

There's cold comfort in the insight one sometimes hears at support group from people farther along the journey. They'll listen to the stories of the new members whose parents are in the early stages of the disease—parents who are still driving, still living alone, still in charge of their own finances, still defiant that nothing is wrong—and then share the wisdom that yes, those are tremendously hard issues, but guess what? It gets easier when it gets worse. That is, when your loved one is less independent because the disease has progressively robbed them of more and more of their abilities, less stubborn because their losses are undeniable, less physically fit from falls or other health crises, then, when they're properly beaten down by this relentless disease, you can actually give some care.

I couldn't square wishing that my mother would hurry up and decline with wanting her to be the whole, independent person she once was, but I couldn't maintain the effort it took to pretend that everything was fine for too much longer, either. There were no easy answers, just more hurdles to scramble over, each requiring a slightly new approach or technique. It felt like a sad irony that as the disease stripped away more of the boundaries my mother had carefully erected to bolster the pretense that everything was fine, I got busy establishing my own, however malleable they turned out to be.

7. MANTRA

"Too long a sacrifice," William Butler Yeats writes in his poem, "Easter 1916," "Can make a stone of the heart. Oh when may it suffice?" He alludes to sacrifice much greater than the one I was making, I know. I was not fighting and dying for my country's independence. I was not about to be executed for tyranny. I get that. But I was, a few years into the Alzheimer's journey, seriously wondering how long this could go on, feeling my heart starting to harden a little bit, and asking the questions every caregiver comes to along this journey: Are we there yet? Is this going to go on forever? I was not, needless to say, living in the present moment.

Now might be an acceptable time—not too late, I hope—to tell you that I teach yoga for a living. Aren't yoga teachers supposed to stay in the present? I really do try. I get on my mat every day, but I still find fear, guilt, and dread very alluring landscapes for my wandering thoughts. Only with the greatest discipline can I look at what is right in front of me and pull myself away from a more habitual inclination toward cranky rumination.

One thing that kept me in a state of worry was how to supply my mother with sufficient company and stimulation.

Though current research into Alzheimer's disease celebrates the person-centered model of care that tries to build on the person's abilities rather than their deficits, it is hard to cherish the very skills that keep undermining your efforts. If socialization is one of the ways to keep your loved one engaged in the world, but your loved one is socially adept enough to say, "No thanks, I'd rather be alone," you find yourself in a bind. I ultimately had to override my mother's claims and tried to sign her up for an excellent program in our community called Adult Day Health. It offers social time, mild exercise, physical therapy, a meal, and extraordinarily friendly faces to anyone with physical or cognitive decline. The program runs from 10 a.m. to 2 p.m., five days a week, with extended hours for those with extra needs. It was perfect, but not yet. Right solution, wrong timing.

Besides her peripatetic nature and general good health—qualities that set her apart from some in her age bracket—my mother had another noteworthy feature for a 75-year-old: she didn't have much gray hair. She combed her thin, gently permed hair neatly, parting it with a comb, smoothing down any loose ends. She hated that it was so thin and always said of any young man with thick, curly hair, "Why did he get that hair? That's not fair." She'd say that to their faces, too, and sometimes reach out to pat it. But for all her complaining about its texture, she was pleased and proud that her hair hadn't gone gray. It became an impediment to certain kinds of social engagement, however, because she didn't see herself as "one of those old people." She didn't have gray hair, after all, so it should have been obvious to me and everyone else that she didn't belong at a program like Adult Day Health. Twice we visited the program and began the paperwork, but both times she refused to go back. She dropped the topic so thoroughly that it almost seemed like she was remembering never to mention it again.

On the up side, she did agree to try out a different day program offered by the Alzheimer's Society called "Staying Connected." This one met just one day a week, from 11 to 2, in a small, bright conference room that sat about 12 people. Applying no pressure at all, I gambled on a tactic my mother used with me when I was five, when she told me that if I didn't like kindergarten after the first week, I wouldn't have to go back. My father thought she was crazy, but she knew I was ready and that I just needed to get past my initial resistance. It worked. I went to kindergarten and liked it so much I spent the next 25 years in school. It worked for my mother, too. She went to the Staying Connected group and told me many times after, "It's such a nice group. And there are some men there, too!"

The Staying Connected group gave my mother one weekday activity. The rest of her time was wide open. Our routine included taking walks every Tuesday, Thursday, Saturday, and Sunday, and now, since selling the car, I took her shopping, took her to appointments, and took her (and her dog) to the vet. Other things might come up, and I was the one to handle it. Calling a washing machine repair guy and being there for his visit and giving the go-ahead to buy a new washer. Arranging the lawn service. Finding someone to rebuild part of her rotting front deck. Calling a painter. Getting someone to come out and clean her gutters. Calling Vicki, the woman who made house calls to cut and perm my mom's hair, then calling again to reschedule if my mom had forgotten and gone for a walk when Vicki arrived. Rescheduling other appointments after my mom canceled them. Taking over her medisets. Getting her taxes done. Getting keys made when she lost hers. Reinstating her credit cards after she'd cancelled them. Counting beer bottles in her trash can. It was a lot, but still nothing like the time commitment living with my mother would require, I reminded myself guiltily. About a quarter of the people who went to support group lived with their demented parent either in the parent's home or their own. How they did it is beyond my comprehension, but I still knew that I was getting a bit fried.

In my yoga practice I came across the concept of *japa*, the repetition of a mantra or prayer. The mantra can be spoken in a low voice, mumbled, or it can be repeated internally, to keep the mind focused. If you've ever tried seated meditation, you know how likely it is that after about four seconds, your mind has moved from the steady flow of your breath to what you're going to have for dinner to that story your colleague told you about her plumbing problem to how annoying it is that someone let a plastic kid's pool blow down the street in the wind storm last night. The mind is amazingly hard to reign in. *Japa* is meant to give the mind a focus, like a stick you'd give an elephant to carry through the market to prevent it from reaching its trunk into every stall.

At some point in my renewed quest to bring in outside caregivers, probably after hearing some sage wisdom at support group, I came up with a mantra to deal with my mom's rejection of my efforts: "I know this is hard for you. I know it's not easy for you to accept that you need help with some things, and I know it's not easy to have to pay for that help. But this is something you need to do. This is something I need." It addressed what I considered to be the highlights of our situation: my mom's increasing needs, her rejection of all my efforts to help her meet them, her unwillingness to pay for help and her subsequent calls to the bank to cancel checks, and growing desperation. Who could argue with all that? It didn't exactly roll off the tongue, though, so I shortened it to: "I know this is hard for you, but it's something we need to do. I need it." State and repeat, state and repeat. If my mother was locked in a world of repetition, then that was the world I had to embrace and come up with my own loop de loops. I had to say it out loud to my mom, but what I really needed to do was say it continually to myself. *Japa*.

This wasn't as easy as it sounds because the mantra had that complicated word that caught in my throat. Need. My mother could not admit that she needed help, and it turned out that I was not much better at it myself. Complaining, sure. I could do that. But saying that I needed help felt like taking off my clothes in the cereal aisle—an eyebrow-raising response to granola. What kind of daughter hires strangers to visit and take walks with her mother when she has time and legs and could do it herself? And too revealing. Who was I to have needs? I wasn't the one with Alzheimer's. I had a full and happy life. A husband, a son, and two dogs. What did I have to complain about?

When you find yourself running full tilt on the hamster wheel of guilt and self-recrimination, it's time to pick up and reread key bits of the always straightforward *The 36-Hour Day*. It's cheerful but not smarmy. It tells you things you either already know and need to hear again or are about to find out. Like, "When a family is able to arrange for someone to stay at home with the person, the person who has dementia may fire the sitter or housekeeper, may be angry or suspicious, may insult her, may refuse to let her in" (315). Check. And then, as if reading my mind and taking hold of my hand to guide me forward, it says: "Be prepared for a period of adjustment. People who have dementia adjust to change slowly: it may take a month for such a person to accept a new program. When you are already exhausted, arguments over respite care may seem overwhelming. You may feel guilty about forcing your relative to do this so that you can get a break" (316). Forget "may." You will. But do it anyway.

Possibly because Alzheimer's and other forms of dementia appear to be far from being "cured," and because treatments and interventions depend so much on the individual patient, conferences and seminars on "dementia" are often more about the caregivers. Attending one of these gives you ample opportunities to hear again and again, in straightforward as well as alarming ways, to take care of yourself. Don't be the caregiver who dies before the one receiving care! Take care of yourself! Caregivers are depressed! Caregivers gain weight and get diabetes! Being a caregiver for a person with dementia will cause so much stress in your life that you'll suffer dementia-like symptoms! It's practically contagious! Take care of yourself! The insistence with which they stress the dangers to caregivers is matched by their fervent hope that we'll do something about it.

At a talk specifically about depression and caregiving, and how important it was that the depressed caregiver get diagnosed and treated, I asked, not with glibness but with a feeling of doom, "And then what? If caregiving is what's causing the depression, and you get treated, but you still have to give care for an open-ended amount of time . . . ?" The question alone shot my stress level through the roof. I needed to get out of there and start taking care of myself! Obviously the answer isn't to simply treat the depression but to avoid it in the first place. Come up with strategies that keep you out of the slough of despond. Put ropes on the bank so you can pull yourself out if you happen to stumble in.

Swami Satchidananda, one commentator on the yoga philosophy contained in *Patanjali's Yoga Sutras*, enjoins the reader to stay in the fray. "To go into a corner and say a mantram is easy *sadhana* [practice]. Anyone can do it. But if we are insulted and keep a serene mind, it is higher than saying thousands of rosaries of *japa*" (148). There may be certain kinds of caregivers, perhaps those who are hell bent on enlightenment during this incarnation, who would like to hear his advice that "if anybody hurts our feelings, we should just smile at them. We should say, 'Thank you . . . Bring your friends also to inflict pain'" (147). There may only be a small market for this kind of recommendation. I prefer the frank, caregiving-centric advice in *Sutra* II.16 that says, "The pains that are yet to come can be and are to be avoided."

Repeating my mantra—"I know this is hard for you, but it's something we need to do. I need it"—didn't help me avoid all future pain, but it gave me some better body armor for the battles ahead. It took me out of the role of the wretched supplicant, always asking my mother to accept more help and being shot down by her scoffing looks and flat out rejection, and put me into the role of the decider, of a sort. It moved our relationship closer to the reverse parent-child model, farther from one in which I could expect to talk things through with her, or share our mutual fears and sadness. The new role made room for compassion, "I know this is hard for you," but it kept us moving in the right direction: "it's something we need to do."

Yogic and Buddhist texts begin with the admission that pain and suffering exist, no question. Yoga teachers often use *Sutra* II:16 to draw attention to the idea that pain and suffering reside in that space between how things really are and our thoughts about how they should be. Some commentators say that pain—especially physical pain—is unavoidable in life, but suffering, the creative spin our mind performs once it gets a hold of the pain, is what we can actually avoid. Who hasn't seen the first gray hair or wrinkle and envisioned frumpy doom? We remember how we used to be, or we project how badly we might turn out. Both paths lead to suffering.

The pain of Alzheimer's and all its losses is not an imaginary projection. It's real. The person with the disease loses independence and eventually their mind. You lose the person or relationship you loved, whatever it was, whether close and loving or distant and convenient, and because you're the caregiver, you lose a bit of your independence, too. To avoid the suffering, we have to feel the pain as it is but not let it take over and color everything we see.

My Alzheimer's-ridden mother is actually an excellent role model in this way. One minute she's telling me that her back hurts, and the next minute she's gasping at how beautiful the clouds are, asking me if I see in them that dog's nose or that bird's wing. She displays wonder and appreciation unselfconsciously, forgetting all about her pain. Repetition is somehow replaced and everything is fresh and new. Without the continuity memory provides, she is unable to make the pain in her back the basis of all future suffering. What suffering? Look at those clouds!

8. PRESERVED CAPABILITIES

Ask most people how long a marathon is and they'll say, "Long!" or maybe the more factual answer, "Twenty-six miles." Ask my mother, and at a time when she'd already forgotten major pieces of her life story, she'd answer, "Twenty six miles, three hundred and eighty five yards." This was one of those odd bits of information she was able to retain, probably because she'd run one.

Research in the field of caregiving has an amusing way of making mundane concepts sound more highfalutin than they really are. One piece of common sense wisdom turned academic gold is this: meaningful activities are an important non-pharmacological treatment for dementia patients. If the goal is to maintain your loved one's function as long as possible and keep her engaged in the world, then you want to find ways to keep her as active as you can within the limits of her abilities. Lack of stimulation is not only painful to observe—who wants to see their loved one hollowed out by purposelessness—but it leads to greater dependence on you, the caregiver. In seeking out these "meaningful activities," you can look at the care receiver's "preserved capabilities." What they still know, what they can still do. If you tap the right vein, it's a win-win: a familiar and meaningful activity for the one you're caring for and a brief break from wondering "what next?" for you.

In the early to middle stages of the disease, my mother couldn't run marathons anymore or even jog to the corner, but she could still walk. Walking was 100% one of her preserved capabilities. She was also very social, though if pressed she'd say she was a loner, didn't really need people, never felt lonely. But put her on a trail with a few strangers, especially strangers with babies and dogs, and right away she'd be bending at the waist to get her head down into the stroller, smiling, introducing herself and our dogs. And she liked to tell her stories—how Doozy got her name, about running a marathon, how she'd hiked the Grand Canyon. You would think that hiring a caregiver to take my mom for walks would be a way to tap right into my mom's preserved capabilities, stave off purposelessness, keep her active, and give me a break.

The problem was that walking—the very capacity I was trying to leverage to bring in other caregivers to lighten my load—was so well preserved that she did an end run around all my planning. She tried to exhaust a few of the caregivers I hired for her in the early days by setting off on five-mile walks, trying to exhaust them. And because walking was all she initially allowed them to do with her, she'd turn them away at the door if she had already walked that day, or thought she had, or just said she had in order to get rid of them.

Skirmishes like these made me throw up my hands in despair, and caregiving manuals like *A Dignified Life: The Best Friends(TM) Approach to Alzheimer's Care*, or *Learning to Speak Alzheimer's* didn't help. Too often these books seem to be giving advice from the far side of the struggle, the side where education, acceptance, and wisdom have all coalesced and caregiving becomes nothing but an extended period of grace, complete with a Sarah McLachlan soundtrack. These books aren't scolding, exactly, but because they report on best practices and "successful strategies" from the winning side of the battle, they didn't help me when I consulted them from my position in the trenches. In fact, they just made me mad. I couldn't treat my mother like my "best friend" because one, she wasn't, and two, I needed my best friend to hear me out when I wanted to complain about my mother. With my best friend, I could refer back to what happened last week; I could share complex trains of thought; I could initiate conversations that wouldn't be derailed and forgotten. I could disagree. I could ask challenging questions. My best friend didn't ask, "Everything is good?" with a look on her face or a tone in her voice that told me only "yes" would do for an answer. With my mother, I had more shared history, genetics, and yes, love, but those didn't add up to "best friend." Our conversational terrain was shrinking fast and we were often at odds. Whether the advice came from books or support group, I really couldn't stomach hearing, "You always have to be patient," or "If you're in a good mood, your loved one will be in a good mood, too," or "Cherish every moment." Honestly.

It was at about this same time in our journey—post car, but before I could convince her to accept the help of outside care-givers—when my mom decided that she didn't want to burden me any more than she had to and that she could get around on her own. I knew she could walk to the four stores within a two-mile radius of her house, but she also insisted she could take our community's specialized transportation service farther afield. This small conveyance, bigger than a minivan but smaller than a bus, takes seniors and people with disabilities from point A to point B for little or no charge. We used it for my mother's return from her weekly Staying Connected meetings at the Alzheimer's Society, but I'd never had her take it to a destination. Going home was one thing. The people at the Alzheimer's Society would see her onto the bus, and the bus driver would see her to her door. Going to an appointment from her house was another thing altogether. But trusting in my mom's claims about yet another preserved capability, I called and scheduled a ride to get her to her next doctor's appointment.

I didn't know that my mom's use of the transportation service hadn't worked out as planned until several months after the fact, when I stopped to chat with one of my mom's neighbors. I commented on a project he had going on in his driveway, and that reminded him, belatedly, to give me the phone number of a man who'd driven my mom home when she'd been lost out by the lake. Imagine Lady Grantham on Downton Abbey, pretending to her butler that she already knew that Mary had been at a Liverpool hotel with Tony Gillingham, and you'll have some idea of the expression on my face as this well-meaning but tardy neighbor relayed the news about my mother being found by a stranger.

Sometimes caregivers have to take on the role of detective. As far as I could piece together, my mom had taken the specialized transportation to her doctor's office, but instead of walking into the building and checking in for her appointment, she had turned around and walked right back out, through the parking lot, down the road, across the freeway overpass, and then four zigzagging miles southeast to a neighborhood hemmed in by Lake Whatcom. When she walked through the kind Samaritan's yard, he asked her how she was doing, where she was heading, and if she needed a ride. Oh no, she insisted, she was just on her way to Fred Meyer. But Fred Meyer was about two miles in the opposite direction. He probably thought it unlikely that she would be going to the store on foot, and somehow talked her into letting him drive her home. Once to her street, my safety-minded mother directed the stranger to leave her at the end of the block, thanked him, and walked the rest of the way home. The man then knocked on a neighbor's door and told his story, gave his name and number, and asked that the neighbor tell my mother's caregiver about this misadventure.

The several months' delay in receiving this information didn't make a huge difference in my caregiving, as it turned out, because my mother never mentioned taking specialized transportation on an out-going journey again, and not knowing about the incident at all, I didn't "catastrophize." I scheduled her appointments for times when it was convenient for me to take her, so the ride and the detour after it didn't recur.

The first time I heard about wandering as a behavioral symptom of Alzheimer's was at an excellent care-partner support program run by our local Alzheimer's Society. Each fall they have 20 pairs of caregivers and care receivers attend a ten-week education and support program. The first part of the morning had all of us in one room, then we'd break into two groups: caregivers in one room, receivers in the other. I have no solid knowledge of what topics the care receivers discussed, though my mom did report to me one time that "an old man put his hand on a lady's leg." In the caregivers' meetings we kept our hands to ourselves and covered everything from how dementia is the umbrella term that includes all the specific forms of cognitive impairment to looking ahead to, and beyond, the loved one's death. Spouses have a completely different entry into and experience on the Alzheimer's journey, and I was (and am) humbled by the love and devotion so many of these caregivers exhibited.

It was one of these long-married, devoted wives who told how her husband got away. He left his bed one night, put on her slippers, and got out the front door despite whatever safety mechanism she had put in place. When she discovered him missing, some inner voice told her where he'd gone. Amazingly, he'd traversed several steep blocks in his wife's bedroom slippers to arrive at his childhood home. He was found standing outside it. This is what I thought wandering was: a middle of the night escape, some mysterious homing mechanism at play, and inappropriate footwear. I had no reason to think my mother had or would wander. She was a walker, not a wander-er.

Then I found this passage in *The 36-Hour Day*: "Wandering may result from being disoriented or getting lost. Sometimes a person sets out on an errand, such as going to the store, makes a wrong turn, becomes disoriented, and becomes completely lost trying to find his way back" (220). I couldn't not see it anymore. Wasn't that exactly what happened to my mother? Wrong turn, disoriented, trying to find her way back? Now I saw "walking" differently. Just like that, my mother had taken on a new behavioral symptom. I had to admit that she'd wandered. But I still chose to ignore the bible's accompanying pronouncement that "a person who has begun to wander away from home or gets lost running errands should no longer live alone. This is a signal to you to make a safer living arrangement for the person" (220).

I still hadn't disabled the stove, taped down area rugs, or replaced her bathtub-shower with a walk-in unit. She had stairs. She had three modes of entrance and egress, and she owned and operated sharp knives. I had stolen as many candles as I could get my hands on, but Fred Meyer still sold them, so she could resupply. I did pocket her matches. The truth is, she still had too many preserved capabilities, she didn't want to move, and I lacked sufficient powers to cajole. My mother had wandered, yes, but she continued to live alone.

There's a concept that gets thrown around in support group occasionally that might seem better suited to a discussion of child rearing than caring for a parent: "natural consequences." A person at group says, "My father refuses to get new shoes, even though the old ones are wearing out." If the father in question is making the transition from "normal aging" into the early stages of Alzheimer's, you might well say, "Fine. Let him live with the consequences." He's stubborn. He's cheap. He hates shopping. Whatever. Let him live with the consequences of wearing those ratty old shoes, and when he gets a blister, or is embarrassed to wear them in front of his friends, he'll finally agree to get a new pair. You might raise other questions, as well: are the old shoes doing any real harm? Does it really matter? This line of questioning drills right down into the heart of caregiving, and in this way does relate to an often heard mantra in childrearing: choose your battles. Is it really worth wrangling over the shoes?

You can see how the idea of natural consequences becomes a part of the caregiver's thinking early on. First, the one you're caring for may indeed be cognizant enough to make his or her own decisions about how s/he wants to spend her time, what to eat, with whom to socialize. You may think it would be better for your mom to continue volunteering at the food bank, cut out processed foods and beer, and call her friends more often, but if she's able to walk, shop, and generally keep a tidier house than you do, who are you to say?

"Natural consequences" might also be a favorite paradigm of caregivers in the early to middle stages of the disease because of the description one often hears about the Alzheimer's sufferer "reversing" in age. Some will argue that a person with dementia goes through the stages of development backwards, losing skills and abilities in the same order and at about the same rate as a baby and growing child acquire them. So if you'd tell a four-year-old, "If you throw Mr. Giraffe at your brother's head again, you're getting a time out," you might think the same would work for your demented mother: "If you don't let the home health care aid in when she comes over to give you your morning meds, your heart rate might go up and your cholesterol will get out of whack."

But the "consequences" approach doesn't work in this case for a variety of obvious reasons: First of all, your mother might not remember what you said two seconds after it left your mouth. Second, she sure isn't going to remember it next Wednesday. Third, you can write all the notes you want and post them around the house—"Health aid bringing meds. Open the door and let her in. Take your meds. Meds are important"—and she'll either take down the notes as soon as you leave or read them over and over but not know how they apply to her.

At some point in the progression of the disease, probably sooner than you'd like, the "natural consequences" approach has to be retired. To say of a middle-stage dementia sufferer, "She won't take her meds! Fine! Let her live with the consequences," is to say, "I'm aware of a huge problem and I'm not doing anything about it."

This, as far as I can understand, is why they call it the "burden" of caregiving. You have to throw out all the logic-based, cause-and-effect-oriented solutions that may have worked in the past and get creative with the new normal. To the questionable claim the person with dementia might make, like, "I can do that myself," the caregiver has to resist saying, "Okay, fine" and try moving in a new direction, toward, "How about we do it together?" For my mom, that worked for tasks like cutting up a cantaloupe, finding items around her house, or going to the store. She claimed she could do them on her own, but I knew otherwise.

When it came to taking walks, however, she could do them on her own, and no amount of walking with her seemed to slake her thirst for more.

9. DECISIONAL CAPACITY

Five months before my mom got lost a second time, I read *The Caregiver's Path to Compassionate Decision Making* by Viki Kind, a bioethicist and child of a parent with dementia. Kind presents a rubric for helping make decisions for a parent that includes the questions: "Does the person have the ability to make his or her own decisions? Does she have decisional capacity?" She writes that if the answer to that is, "it fluctuates," or "no," then the next question should be, "How old is the person developmentally? What is her mental age?" The point of this exercise is to arrive at a more solid ground for decision making.

If you wouldn't think it necessary to control everything your 16-year-old eats, then maybe it follows that you shouldn't feel compelled to boss your mom into eating certain things, either. If it's developmentally appropriate to monitor what your seven-year-old is doing in the kitchen, then maybe you should be equally vigilant of a parent who seems to be operating at that developmental age. The "reverse aging" model has its problems, for sure, but Kind tries to use it in a way that honors both the caregiver's and the care receiver's situation. I took it as a framework for helping me pick my battles.

At support group over the years, I have heard many people ask about issues related to food: what the parent is or isn't eating, how much, how often, and what to do about it. For quite a while, these concerns seemed overblown. I was more into the "natural consequences" mindset in those early years, thinking that if the person didn't want to eat, that was their choice. If they wanted to eat only ice cream, fine! Kind's rubric for determining "decisional capacity" gave me a new way of understanding how to assess certain needs and risks.

What's so interesting about dementia and the human brain is that capacities do not decline and vanish at the same rate. While the disease trajectory can be mapped very broadly to show what awaits most sufferers, it cannot accurately pinpoint where anyone will be at any specific time. My mother's geriatrician had suggested I remove my mom's stove at a point in her decline when, I suppose, many other caregivers would have seen a great risk at leaving a functional stove in their parent's home. But years past that point, my mother could still fry up a hamburger for her dinner. *The 36-Hour Day* said frankly that once a person wanders or gets lost on errands, it's time to move them into a more protected environment. But my mother could still vacuum, do laundry, garden, and make her bed with crisp, tight, military-grade corners. She had no clear memory of how often she went to the store or what she bought, but she could still get there on foot, write checks, and make it home. On many days her functional skills—her ability to take care of her activities of daily living—looked more intact than mine.

When I started paying more attention to, and worrying about my mother's diet, I noticed that she tended toward two flavors: salty and sweet. Along with her 12-pack she'd buy a rotisserie chicken, potato chips, ice-cream, cantaloupe, yogurt, and cookies. She also, to her credit, bought bags of pre-made salads, but these often went bad before I discovered them in her produce drawer. She talked about all the baked potatoes she'd make for herself, but unbaked potatoes piled up. She talked about making enchiladas and other two- or three-step meals, but I never found evidence that she had done that. Sometimes I came over and found her eating ice cream out of the half-gallon container; sometimes she had chips and cantaloupe for breakfast. Eventually I became one of the hand-wringing people at support group who talked about what her parent was eating, but mostly I remained the sole support group attendee who talked about what my mother drank.

Outside of support group, responses to accounts of my mother's drinking ranged from "oh well" to "oh my god." The "oh well" camp was populated by those who could imagine wanting to drink away their sorrows in old age, too, who didn't think they were in a position to cast the first stone. The "oh my god" group couldn't believe I let it happen. In between were most of the people at support group who knew it was a problem but understood that, given my mom's functional abilities, it was difficult to curtail. Unless she breaks her leg, I'd say grimly, there's no chance she'll stop walking to the store. I was right. She fell and broke her wrist during that period, but an arm cast wasn't enough of a handicap to keep her home.

During this time when my mother held steady and nothing I could say or do made a dent in her drinking, I was at least successful at bringing in a caregiver who accompanied her on two-hour walks on Mondays and Fridays, and another one who charmed my mom into letting her just "visit" every Wednesday afternoon, something my mother had told me she never wanted. "I don't want anyone to just sit there at look at me," was how she'd put it. Maybe the Wednesday caregiver averted her eyes when they visited; maybe she never actually sat down. She showed up in flowing skirts and heavy jewelry and would hug my mom frequently. Though she was unlike my mom in almost every way, it somehow worked out.

I hoped that the structure these visits provided would help balance out her progressively lopsided cravings, and with a little less worry about my mom, I got back to one of my obsessive pleasures: planning my family's next adventure.

I signed us up for a week-long Sierra Club service trip at Mt. Rainier and started working on getting into shape. We'd be at high elevation, carrying heavy bags, doing who knew what kind of service. We took a few day-long hikes in July to ready ourselves, then packed our backpacks and trained a little bit more. I was looking forward to staying on Mt. Rainier for a whole week and absorbing the sights, sounds, and smells of that beautiful environment, and being away from the internet, phones, and caregiving. As the trip approached, I made sure my mother had all the basics covered, and I felt excited and happy.

Then, on the Friday afternoon before our Saturday morning departure, I got a call from a man telling me not to worry, my mother was fine. He'd just dropped her off at her house after finding her wandering through his neighborhood three miles away. "She's fine," he repeated. "Just thought you should know."

What I didn't know at the time was that eventually things were going to get better because in that instant they had just gotten a whole lot worse.

I pieced together that she'd gone on a routine walk to the grocery across the freeway and bought her regular 12-pack and chicken combo. I figured that she'd left the store and turned the wrong direction for home, heading west instead of east. As is reported in the literature about wandering, once on the wrong track, she didn't stop to ask for help and kept walking in a fairly straight line, going as far west as she could go before land's end. I also discovered that she'd written the Good Samaritan a check for $2.00 for his trouble. That was my mom: still thoughtful, still cheap.

Crises have a way of bringing everything into focus. Once I understood what had happened—that my mother had gotten lost on a routine and habitual outing—I knew I'd arrived at one of those lines in the sand I'd drawn around safety. This couldn't continue. When her meds had become a confounding mess, I got her a mediset and gave her one day's meds at a time. When driving seemed dangerous for her and everyone else, we sold the car. Now even walking was presenting a danger, but short of stealing all her shoes or putting her into a locked facility, I couldn't imagine a way to keep her from taking walks whenever she wanted to.

Though my mother couldn't remember very many details about the day, she knew something scary had happened and her anxiety softened her up a bit. Same for me. I felt, for perhaps the first time, how truly vulnerable she was. My first impulse was to hug her and help her feel safe again, but deeper down I felt like the rug had been pulled out from under us, and I questioned how safe she could ever really be again. I had a momentary loss of faith in my own efforts, feeling like I'd been doing nothing but setting things in place to give the semblance of normalcy and stability, all the while ignoring the real and precarious world my mother actually lived in. As I tried, for my own sense of order and logic, to draw out her side of the story, what I mostly got was a clearer view of her confusion. Her defenses were down for a time, and in that tender reunion a tiny gap opened up and I stepped through. On that new terrain a solution presented itself. Was I taking advantage? In that moment of mutual relief I got her to agree that I should take over her checkbook, and that from then on, I'd be the one to manage her money and take her shopping.

It was huge. Bigger than foisting caregivers on her, bigger even than selling her car. But badly timed. I was supposed to be heading off to Mt. Rainier the next morning, not downgrading my mother's decisional capacity a notch or two. Not taking away more of her independence—and certainly not giving up more of mine.

A lot happened that Friday night. First, I went home and cried. I cried for my mother's situation, but also for myself. I had been looking forward to the trip to Mt. Rainier for so many reasons, and now, because my mother wandered from such a familiar path, it was impossible for me to leave. Or was it? What if I stocked her refrigerator with food for the week, brought in caregivers who could visit one or two times a day, and arranged to have someone bring her two beers every day? Why would she need her checkbook if all of those needs were being met? But could I live with myself if I left my mother for a week immediately after this traumatic incident? Another voice was equally insistent. Could I keep doing this caregiving work indefinitely if I didn't?

Within 24 hours of admitting that my mother had become a bona fide wanderer, I tweaked our trip plans so that my husband and son would leave as planned on Saturday morning and I'd drive down by myself on Monday. I used my extra days at home to plan for every possible wrinkle that could arise from this new arrangement. I contacted a local home-care agency and set up multiple visits for every day of the coming week; filled my mother's refrigerator with easy-to-eat, sweet and salty foods; ordered a Safe Return bracelet and made a dog tag with an emergency phone number for my mom to wear until it arrived; asked my sisters-in-law to be on call; and asked my mom's neighbor if she'd mind bringing two beers to my mom every afternoon.

When you care for someone with dementia, you have to develop a thick skin around the whole "what people will think" concern. I have come to the studied conclusion that people think all kinds of crazy nonsense, so the answer to "What will they think?" has to be, "Who cares?" My mother's neighbor signed on and showed up every afternoon that week with two ice cold Alaskan Ambers.

The trip to Mt. Rainier worked out as well as it could have given the events preceding it, and my mother survived the week just fine. She didn't get lost a third time, she ate the food I'd left her, she accepted the hired company, and she was thrilled at the delivery of two beers every afternoon. The only thing that upset her was that she didn't know where her checkbook was. Had I seen it?

Agreements made with a person suffering from dementia have short shelf lives. I knew that going in. Within days of the wandering incident, my mom went back to her well worn habit of writing a shopping list and planning, if I can use that word, her trip to the store. But in getting ready, she would discover, several times a day, every day, for at least a year, that she couldn't find her checkbook. I'm sure she spent hours looking for it, which must have been tremendously frustrating for her, and then she'd call to ask if she'd left it in my car, or under my kitchen table. Then she'd ask me to call one of the ladies who visited her. Maybe they'd seen it. In one way this was nothing new. She'd been calling about her lost purse for years. Now, however, we knew the exact location of what she was looking for. It was in my desk drawer. Like Johnny Carson's Carnac the Magnificent, holding a card to his forehead and divining the answer before even hearing the question, I could predict who was calling and already know my response.

Finding out that we had her checkbook over and over did not solve the problem, however, because the new normal hadn't settled in and upset her every time. Telling my mom that I had her checkbook and that I was happy to take her to the store took us back a few squares to a scoffing, "You don't have to do that," or "I always walk on my own," and, with heat and anger, "I want my checkbook back. Now." Click. I hadn't been hung up on since selling her car. What was my mantra? Now was the time to play, repeat, play, repeat. "I know this is hard for you, but . . ." It was hard, no question, but I had applied a new metric to the situation, a "how would I feel if . . ."

measure of accountability. How would I feel if I let my mother have her checkbook back and she resumed her old habit of walking to the store and got lost again? How negligent would I feel if yet another stranger called to tell me my mom had been wandering down his street, clearly distressed? How careless would that be?

It would be careless, all right, and lucky for us, the Bellingham police department was on our side. One afternoon my mom called and we went through the whole script, from the fake, cheery optimism I mustered to say, "Hi Mom, how are you?" to her familiar closing, "I want my checkbook." During these calls she might also throw in, for variety, "You have no right," or "I'll call the police." By this point in the conversation I usually lost my good cheer, and I probably said on more than one occasion, "Fine! Go ahead!" It's hard to know what will "stick" with a person suffering dementia—what little bit of information will take hold and what will pass right through. This idea of calling the police stuck, apparently, because one afternoon when my husband went over to visit he found a police car in her driveway. She'd made good on her word, and safety-check bonus points, she still knew how to dial 9-1-1.

She had called the police to report that her daughter had taken her checkbook, and the police dispatched an officer to investigate. It didn't go as my mother had hoped. Apparently the officer got a pretty clear grasp of the situation, and Paul's account of the who, what, where, when, and why all assured the officer that there was no theft, only filial duty hard at work. We learned then that my mom's call to the police was actually helpful because it put her on their radar as a person to watch out for. If she called again, they'd know her story.

The happier side effect of taking the checkbook was that now I could control how much beer she drank. I decided that two beers a day was a reasonable amount—not as friendless as one, not as decadent as nine—and I worked hard to keep my word. I kept a stash in my Prius so that I could always make my delivery; I bought it for the caregivers so they could make theirs. My screening questions for caregivers now included this litmus test: are you willing to bring two beers? Teetotalers need not apply. Whoever took the afternoon shift had to be the supplier.

At a support group one night, a woman talked about how her mother had taken to drinking gin and how no one could stop her. The mother still lived alone, was still fit, and could go to the store whenever she wanted to. I listened sympathetically then offered my story, for whatever it was worth—one possible way to deal with a seemingly intractable situation. Another woman talked to me after group, asking more detailed and desperate questions about "how I'd done it." How any of us do what we do is a bit murky and mysterious, but in this case, I might have said that the solution "did" itself. While I can't apply the "natural consequences" framework to my mother anymore, I still feel its sway. I couldn't live with the constant worry her frequent trips to the store and her drinking were causing, and the opportunity to make a change presented itself. I took it.

As for my mother's "decisional capacity" and mental age, sometimes I think of her like one of those 5-year-olds you read about in the newspaper who somehow manage to drive the family car sixteen miles before hitting a tree or who sneak onto an airplane and fly to Milwaukee. How do they do it? Sheer will seems to outstrip any capacity for logic or planning, and somehow they survive without a scrape.

10. BEING IN CHARGE

A couple years after a flurry of putting in new garden beds, stone pathways, and rock walls, my garden definitely began to show signs of neglect. An invasive vine crept in, my plant combinations didn't work out so well, and the whole thing needed a trim. My mother helped me with a lot of the initial work to get the garden going, and she would probably still offer to come help me with it any time I asked. Her garden got to looking a little wild, too, and as we pulled into or out of her driveway—no matter what season—she'd look at her front yard and say, "Someday I'm going to come out here and clean all this up." In the winter I'd remind her that it wasn't really time for gardening. In the spring she'd get distracted by the new growth. In the summer I'd suggest hiring someone to help her. But mostly, because gardening had been a lifelong passion and one of her "preserved capabilities," I left her to it.

It was a pretty low risk, high reward activity for her. She stopped using trimmers or shears and would instead pick off dead leaves or small branches by hand. In every season, often in her pajamas.

Should I have stepped in and done more? Or is it right to let a person with diminishing capacity continue to do what they can?

Back when my mother was showing early signs of mild cognitive impairment and letting things slide a little bit, my husband and I hired a lawn care service that would mow and trim for her every two weeks. Because I knew she'd refuse to pay, we made it our gift. Her first response was a scoffing, "I don't need that," but she grudgingly accepted it. Later she came to really appreciate it and kindly told us so. She even seemed to be able to accept that lawn care, like other out-sourced help, was essential if she wanted to remain at home. Despite her braggadocio when it came to certain competencies, she got that she couldn't do everything on her own. Then a year or more down the road she said something, again, about how much she liked having someone take care of her lawn and added, "You shouldn't have to pay for that," surprising us all by remembering that we did. Taking her at her word—a tricky business when you're dealing with someone with Alzheimer's—I agreed. From then on, I wrote the check from her account, not ours. It gave me one more line item to figure into the calculations I made in the pursuit of balance: how much does it cost to keep her at home? Is it worth it? Will it last?

At home, there are the obvious costs of mortgage, taxes, repair, and maintenance. There are the essential utilities: water, power, sanitation, gas, and electric. Then there are the things you'll pay for one way or the other, like food, phone service, cable. Perhaps all of these can be seen as "one way or the other" costs. An assisted living facility simply bundles up the taxes, maintenance, water, power, etc. and gives you one base fee plus the cost of care on top of that. Living at home simply means getting to make a few more choices about where the money goes. But increasingly, the choices are mine, not my mother's. I am the one in charge. This setup, though advantageous and convenient, is not stress free.

Sometimes I consider the alternatives, or, just for fun, I create distracting fantasies. Had my parents stayed together, one such daydream goes, my father would be the one caring for my mother, presumably, since both his body and mind are in pretty good shape. I would then be an onlooker rather than an overseer. Concerned and still opinionated, I would follow their lives, but not direct them. They would probably still be in Phoenix, where I grew up, maybe in the same small, ranch-style house with its low ceilings and wall-to-wall, green shag carpet. Maybe they'd still have the never-used golden living room furniture; maybe they'd still harvest grapefruit off the 8 trees that grew in the suburban yard that was once part of a fruit orchard. My husband, son, and I would spend a week or two a year basking in the desert heat then return to forested, rainy Bellingham. To flesh out this fantasy of what could have been is to voyage into a parallel universe, one where my father never left her and where every subsequent action in my mother's life never took place. No move to California, no time in a Kentucky Fried Chicken, no "penis on my head" story, no Doozy of a dog, no Bellingham.

Back to reality, I accept that calling my parent's divorce and my mom's subsequent heartbreak "fortuitous" would be going too far, but I see that the silver lining was that in going through the divorce process, my mother got me. At 17, I was too old to be split in any kind of custody ordeal, so she got me in that physical, living-in-the-house way, but she got me in many other lasting ways, too. We were always fairly close, and her despair brought us closer. And if not immediately, because I was under 18 at the time, I eventually became the permanent backup. She named me her Power of Attorney for Healthcare, her Durable Power of Attorney for legal and financial matters, the executor of her will, and a cosigner on her bank account. Having the legal documents stuffed into a safe deposit box for all the years my mother was well was easy. No tasks or responsibilities grew out of being POA or cosigner. I never really thought about the implications of it; it was just one of those things a single, aging parent might do for some future time of need.

At support group this topic comes up a lot, and even though "Review your legal documents" is a bullet point under "Plan Ahead" on the Dementia Information Sheet the local Alzheimer's Society puts out, I've learned that my mother's excellent planning is not the norm. What I took as a matter of course—that my mother had her papers in order and that she'd named me her primary back up—others describe as a goal they are still far from reaching. Many want-to-be caregivers are locked out of their parent's health or financial situation and run into the parent's distrust and denial, two nearly impenetrable barriers to gaining access to the legal "right" that makes certain kinds of caregiving possible. This is not to say that a child can't give care, love, and concern without being a POA or a cosigner; it is simply to say that without those things, that child's ability to make decisions on their parent's behalf is severely limited.

In my situation, as the backup plan got dragged into the foreground, especially after I took over my mom's checkbook, I felt an almost equal mixture of relief and unreasonable guilt. Relief that my mother could no longer buy as much beer as she wanted and that I could take over her bill paying and financial oversight, but guilt—remember, I did say unreasonable—that I was stealing. Having control of someone else's money put me into a new, awkward relationship with my conscience. Going to the bank to cash a check for her, reimbursing myself for an expense I covered, or ordering a new debit card for myself all made me feel the need to turn out my pockets and say, look, I haven't taken anything! Really! Then that line from Hamlet comes to mind—"the lady doth protest too much, me-thinks"—and I'm left with no recourse whatsoever. Try writing the sentence, "I honestly don't steal from my demented mother" and see if you don't feel guilty, too.

It didn't help that my sister and I had argued about the checks my mother sent her, that my mom asked me to buy Christmas and birthday gifts for myself and my family, or that she had no idea how much she was spending on the caregivers that I arranged for her, all of whom she said she didn't need. All of these pricked my feelings of guilt. Who was I to buy my son a $70 dollar robe for his birthday on my mother's behalf? Who was I to question my mother's giving and my sister's receiving? It didn't help that in the infrequent communication I did have with my sister, she'd often say, "Mom seems the same to me," suggesting to my oversensitive ears that I had taken control prematurely. That mom was still the same old mom, and that I was making something out of nothing. I heard, however unreasonably, a soft murmur of accusation. The accusation became louder than a murmur if my mom ever heard how much things cost, so I generally kept all of that to myself.

If I wanted to paint the picture in the broadest strokes, I might say that my mother and I are simply on the opposite side of depression-era awareness. She cleans, saves, and reuses Saran wrap. Though I reduce and recycle in myriad ways, saving Saran wrap isn't one of them. She always clipped coupons, watched for sales, and would ask for rain checks if the sale item was out of stock. Though I reuse holiday wrapping paper and buy clothes second hand, I don't refuse to pay the higher price of organic food because it's "ridiculous." I have accepted the fact that some skilled gardening helpers charge up to $35 an hour, whereas my mother, in the early stages of Alzheimer's, cancelled a check she herself had written when she decided after the fact that $300 was too much to pay for the garden work that had already been done. She had always been frugal, and now, beginning to reoccupy memories from a time in her life when gas only cost ten cents a gallon, she was getting downright cheap. I didn't love it, but once I understood the going rate, I didn't think it scandalous to pay a stranger between $18-25 an hour to come walk with her, but I knew she would.

Taking over my mother's finances meant adjusting to our different world views, but it also meant hiding things that I knew she wouldn't be comfortable with. Was that lying, or did it mean I was being a responsible caregiver? Support group affirms the latter, but the tension exists just the same.

After about a year of controlling my mother's checkbook, as I got into the rhythm of being the go-to person for my mother's finances, including putting as many bills as possible on auto-pay, getting my address on accounts so that checks and bills came to me, and beginning to look at the status of her retirement accounts, it occurred to me one day that I could die at any moment. Not because I was so stressed out, but because freakish and inconvenient things happen. I could be hit by a car. I could go down in a plane. I could swallow a cashew wrong. Also, at this time, I had been volunteering with a local agency as an advance care planning facilitator, so asking hard questions about end-of-life planning had become second nature. "Who will speak for you?" "Who will make decisions on your behalf?" In my volunteer job I was asking primarily about health care decisions, but most people took the opportunity to review all of their documents, which was an excellent outcome of our work.

My mother did have her affairs in order to an exemplary degree, but that question of "who would speak for her" suddenly jumped out at me. If I dropped dead, who would speak for my mother on matters of health and wealth and everything else? Who would step in and keep this highly orchestrated three-ring circus running? My sister. The one who hadn't visited my mother in years, who was dealing with her own physical and mental struggles, and who'd implied a few times that she didn't think my mother was "so bad." At worst she'd enter the picture and disrupt everything I had set in place. At best she'd ask Paul to carry on. Then the burden of delivering care would fall to him, but he wouldn't have any way to pay for it. I couldn't imagine it either way.

To change or update your will is a simple enough, if costly, undertaking when you are of sound mind. When decision making capacity starts to disintegrate, not so much. Suddenly, what had been a leisurely stroll on the path of decline now felt like a relay. Could she still pass the baton? Or would she wander off the track and start collecting rocks?

The lawyer I chose was on a list given out by the Northwest Regional Council on Aging, an organization that could answer any number of questions on issues related to aging, resources, health care, Medicaid, and so on. He did some pro bono work for seniors, and though my mother didn't qualify for free legal assistance, I thought it was a good sign that he was a strong protector of vulnerable citizens' rights. On the way to the lawyer's office my mother kept asking me what appointment we were going to—her doctor? the dentist? When I repeatedly told her we were seeing a lawyer to update her will, she'd say in that vague way that always clued me in to her confusion, "Oh," or more confidently, "Okay, whatever you think. You know what to do."

At the lawyer's office we were seated in the conference room that spoke to the lawyer's charitable nature. On one wall was a sagging bookshelf filled with dusty law journals and on the opposite side of the small room was a simple folding table with a phone, a notepad, and a copy machine. Two desiccated plants threatening to bust out of their pots stood next to the large window overlooking Bellingham's main downtown thoroughfare, and the conference table we sat around was an old oak whose joints seemed to be giving way under the weight of the wood and our arms. The lawyer, a white bearded man with an intense gaze, introduced himself and welcomed us all in, then immediately sent Paul and me out into the hall so he could talk to my mom privately. "That'll be interesting," we said to each other in the hallway, and then, "I wonder what the hell they're talking about," when their tete-a-tete went on for fifteen minutes or so. And then that unreasonable guilt crept in: did the lawyer think we were coercing my mother into something? Who was I to drag her in here to change her will?

Back in the conference room we got down to business, and only gradually, as details became relevant, did I learn what the lawyer and my mom had talked about. Reassuringly, my mother kept saying things like, "Whatever Denise says; she takes good care of me," and I tried to disconnect the tape in my head that kept playing the voice of doubt. I kept it quiet as we got through the main reason for our visit: to change the names of those who'd be POA and executor of the will in the event of my death. Instead of my sister, we put Paul in line as second after me, and we put my mother's sister in line to be third. There. Done. But no, my mother had apparently talked about my brother while we were out in the hallway, and there was a lot more the lawyer wanted to say about inheritance.

Imagine how this scene might play out for those fortunate enough to have a fortune awaiting them. That was not the case for us. If my mother continues to live in relative good health beyond the time she might have to move into a facility, she will run out of money in about six years. Odds say that death after placement comes sooner than that, but given the fact that at this juncture she was only five or six years into her Alzheimer's journey, and in good health, she could live a lot longer. All to say, the whole idea of an inheritance from my mother's estate seemed unlikely, but that didn't dissuade the lawyer from going over every detail with a fine tooth comb.

In my mother's previous will, drawn up about 12 years earlier, she had named all three of her children as equal inheritors of whatever remained in her bank or retirement accounts, but named only my sister and me as inheritors of her house. The house and its contents could be divided by the two of us in any equitable manner we arrived at. I had not proposed changing anything to do with inheritance, so it came as a bit of a surprise that my mom had told the lawyer that she wanted to change her will to leave everything to my sister and me because my brother had been distant to the point of nonexistent (not her exact words). This had come up in their private conversation, apparently, and now the lawyer wanted to ask me about it. Was it true?

It was, as far as I knew, though admitting it felt like a shame that implicated me as much as my brother. No, he had not been a part of my mother's life for the last 10 years or more, as far as I could see, but what did I know? I am as guilty of being out of touch with him as he is with me. All I knew about his health, three marriages, three divorces, children, and pet alligator came from my father, who kept in touch with him and had visited several times in his small southwestern Missouri town. As for my mother, maybe he did call once or twice and she just didn't remember. What she did remember was a hurtful comment he'd made decades earlier, implying that she was to blame for my father leaving her. The whole situation felt pitiful: My husband, my mother, and I sitting around this droopy oak table with the lion-eyed lawyer, describing the threadbare cloth of my family, deciding who would be listed as inheritors of nothing. How had it come to this? And why did I feel guilty again? Why did my mother have two children who didn't visit and spend time with her? Why did one of those two never even send a Mother's Day card? The sadness of it can be overwhelming, so I suppose that forgetfulness can, in some ways, salve the wound.

However fraught the entire episode was, however unflattering a snapshot of me as a sister and us as a family, I was relieved to make the changes we made to my mother's will, and I am comforted to know that my husband will speak for my mother if I drop dead tomorrow. And if I don't predecease her, thanks to the updates she made to her will and their consequent legal requirements, I have a new task: Upon my mother's death, as executor of her will, I am charged with sending my brother a check for one dollar, if even that remains in her estate, to indicate that no, he was not forgotten, just excluded. Such are the pathetic rewards of being the one in charge.

11. UNMET NEEDS

One morning when I went to pick up my mom to take her out, she asked how the party had gone. "What party?" Giving her her morning pills, seeing that she had her keys, putting her coat on, I brushed past the non sequitur. Then, as we waited at a stoplight a few minutes later, she asked again. "How was your party?" I knew enough about dementia care to know that arguing with a demented person about facts—"This is a cold winter." / "Actually it's the warmest on record." "I never see you anymore." / "Yes you do; you saw me last night" —isn't productive. It's best to tune in to the feelings behind the confusion and, when there's no obvious distress or anxiety, you can tie a rope to the nearest tree, grab a headlamp, and head into the cave to find out what's lurking in the depths. "The party you had last night," she added. Even though I know not to dispute the facts, I'm hard wired to do it. "We didn't have a party last night," I said.

Undeterred, maybe a little exasperated at my obtuseness, she went on. "Yes, I was sitting there on your back deck, and there were people all around, but nobody was talking to me, and then Paul came over and said, 'Patty, do you want to go home?' And I said yes, because I was kind of bored, so he took me home. Did everyone stay late? It looked like a nice party." The tip off was "Patty." My husband has never called my mom Patty, he has always known her as Pat. Patty comes from an earlier era and remained a term of endearment for a few, but it was not in regular use. She was Aunt Patty to her sister's children, but visits with them were rare now that they were mostly grown, so she was only Patty in her dimming memories.

Impressed at the level of detail in my mom's recounting, I asked, "Maybe that was a dream?" "No," she said, "Or, I don't think so. I can remember it as clear as day." Rarely has my mother reflected, in real time, on the changes going on in her brain. At most she'll say, "You know I'm losing my mind," or "My brain isn't working right." Mainly she says, "I'm lucky to be so healthy," skipping over her losses entirely. Never, up till that moment, had she told me her thoughts and then allowed me to poke around in them, probing for origins and meaning. Less out of a need to argue than to explore, I suggested that since Paul never called her Patty, maybe she was remembering a different party. Since we are not really party-throwing types, maybe she was recalling an occasion with her far more social sister and brother-in-law. Like her sister's husband, my husband is tall, fair, and a bit of a joker. Both of them have built a relationship with my mom on good natured teasing and humor. "I don't know," she said, "it seems like it happened last night, at your house. That's so strange." Rather than feeling freaked out by this new development, I felt a little surprised, even mildly entertained. This was the first time Alzheimer's had presented me with a behavioral symptom I'd call "fun." Perseverance and resistance, I could do without. But delusions! Those were close cousins to storytelling, fantasy, and dreamscapes. I was ready to dig in.

My mother's memory of the party I never had goes by the delightful name "spontaneous confabulation." Spontaneous because nothing in our conversation or the events of that morning provoked it. The story just welled up on its own.

Some disparate memories spontaneously reconfigured themselves, and out popped this new narrative. Another story she told, that I chalked up to spontaneous confabulation once I learned the term, was of the time she jumped out of an airplane with "that man." The difference between the party story and the parachuting story is that she repeated the latter quite often, whereas the former emerged then disappeared all in the course of a single morning. The parachuting story made appearances at dinners we had together, on walks, and with caregivers. It took on the stature of one of those memorable adventures, something she was proud she'd done, like hiking the Grand Canyon or running a marathon. But she never had. At least, I don't think she had. And besides. What man? If she did jump out of an airplane with a strange man, it must have happened during a time when I was seriously not paying attention.

These and other storytelling incidents reminded me of a woman at support group who recounted sitting at her dad's bedside at the later stages of his disease, listening to a bizarre story about events from his time in the military. Suffering from Lewy Body dementia, her father had experienced hallucinations, delusions, and "fire storms," as another caregiving couple called them, all expressions of distorted or imagined truths. *The 36-Hour Day* explains that "sometimes delusions appear to come from misinterpreting reality. Sometimes they are tied to the person's past experiences." But then it adds parenthetically, "A note of caution: not all odd things people say are delusions" (291). What is the Joseph Heller line? "Just because you're paranoid doesn't mean they aren't out to get you." Turns out, some of her father's ramblings contained actual facts. The daughter had simply never heard them before, and she was much more accustomed to discounting his delusions than finding new truth in his wild stories.

Like that daughter, I, too, had been prone to dismiss a lot of what my mother said. "I see that man every day," she might say of an unremarkable pedestrian as we drove toward the park for our regular Sunday walk. Of two men who resembled each other only to the extent that they both had brown hair and were Caucasian, she observed, "I see those two brothers walking to school together all the time." How did she come up with that? But for all my incredulity, I began to open up to the possibility that I couldn't be so sure. And with the parachuting story, I began to think, "Who am I to say?" If your mother tells you she jumped out of an airplane often enough, you begin to think that maybe she did! You can slip into a strange new reality for a time, or, when you realize that the ultimate truth of the claims doesn't really matter, you can start to live there.

"Provoked" confabulation, on the other hand, represents a more normal or predictable response to faulty memory. Someone might ask, "What did you have for breakfast?" and instead of saying, "I don't remember," you might retrieve a familiar, if inaccurate data set: coffee and toast. Never mind that your grandson took you out to breakfast and that you had an omelet. The more familiar routine pops to mind, and you say what is generally true but not specifically accurate.

My mother has shared many provoked confabulations with me, Paul, and her caregivers, many so convincing that I have often felt like one of the blind men feeling the elephant. In that Jain allegory, six blind men touch a different part of an elephant and come to very dissimilar interpretations of what this creature must be. A pillar, a rope, a snake, and so on. It takes the village wise man to explain that there's no need to argue, that each of them is correct. There are many ways to get to the truth.

One of my favorite provoked confabulations stemmed from a call—completely out of the blue—from my mother's brother, Jim, aka Jimmy, the one who'd been locked outside with my mom by the callous baby sitters. Jimmy, who my mother hadn't seen in more than 20 years. What my mother told me was that Jim and "those girls" were coming to visit the

111

very next weekend, and though she'd invited them to stay with her, she wasn't very happy about it. From my uncle Jim I learned—after I tracked him down and asked him—that he had called my mother to ask if he and a woman friend of his might stop in Bellingham two years hence on their way from Seattle to Vancouver. He assured me that they'd be staying in a hotel for the one night they'd be in town. Respectfully, he was asking way ahead of time, giving her ample warning.

Once I got the dates straight and reassured my mom that no, she didn't have to make up the guest beds or go get snacks and drinks any time soon, I thought the topic would go away. We could resurrect it about 22 months later, much closer to the date of his actual visit. But no, it became one of those mysterious burrs that kept working its way under her saddle, with "those girls" being the focus of her complaint. "What girls?" I'd ask, seeking a way to expand the tight conversational loop. "Who are they and why do they bug you so much?" According to my mom, they were high school students that Jim had brought to Bellingham when they'd all come to attend a local math conference some years ago. All of that was convincing enough. The girls, apparently, had stayed with my mom in her guest room, and they had been very rude. Though she had been a model host, my mother implied in her telling, the girls would come downstairs only to get food and would then march back up the stairs and eat in their room. They came and went but never talked to her.

"Not all odd things people say are delusions," the trusty guide says. Okay, but this one was. Jim had been a high school math teacher, but beyond that, he had never been to Bellingham in the fifteen years we'd lived there, with or without two rude girls in tow. The woman friend Jim said he would be traveling with must have morphed into the two girls, and some unsocial behavior of previous house guests must have lodged itself somewhere deep inside my mother's brain. Did a pair of visitors ever take food up to their room and eat behind a closed door? That was about as far as my amateur detective skills could take me.

If provoked confabulations present tiny strands that can be woven together to form a larger truth, then what this one showed me, like the party story did, was that my mother was experiencing herself as the "orphan girl" once again. Through memory loss, lost autonomy, and loneliness, she was once again that ignored little girl who had the door shut in her face. Here it was, fresh and new, in the form of a party at which no one talked to her and two rude houseguests who didn't want her company. In this way, these inventions spoke as clearly to her central truth as any factual events ever could.

As caregivers we are told to get to the underlying cause of behavioral symptoms, not to be distracted by the symptoms themselves. But once you get to it, then what? Short of providing my mother 24-hour-a-day psychotherapy, I felt ill equipped to address the scars left by her childhood wounds. She had hours of daily activities, attentive caregivers, me, my husband, my son, and my dog. She got attention. Was it enough? Could it ever be enough?

In the Alzheimer's literature you come across the phrase, "unmet needs." These are needs that the caregiver doesn't know exist because the person with dementia cannot express them. Wandering, for example, could stem from the unmet need of having to go to the bathroom. A person might get up out of her chair with the need to relieve herself, but two steps toward the bathroom she finds the front door instead, and off she goes. Or maybe it could stem from boredom, stimulation being the unmet need. A fall could be traced back to the unmet need of hunger. The person can't express that they are hungry, so they don't eat, get light headed, and faint. Some of the unmet needs are obvious: those receiving care need a safe environment, food and drink, and ample opportunities to go to the bathroom and get rest. Our job as caregivers is to see that our loved ones' basic needs are being met. Seems simple enough.

From a wider angle, the concept of "unmet needs" is existentially overwhelming. Consider the need for meaningful engagement, or respect, or love. I understand the intent behind writing these and other needs into a checklist-type "Bill of Rights" for the Alzheimer's sufferer—so that we don't forget the person's essential humanity or start mistaking memory loss and confusion for a lack of sensitivity to the world around them—but I am caught up by the enormity of the challenge. It is a good day for me when I feel fully and meaningfully engaged in my life, when I get a whiff of respect, when I experience unconditional love. Does anyone else know a teenager? Give me ten minutes when all three of those needs are met and I'd be extremely happy. The caregiving manuals that blithely advise readers to address these and other unmet needs of the care receivers, as if it were as simple as getting them toast and yogurt for breakfast, are the ones I've thrown across the room, meeting my urgent need for a self-indulgent tantrum.

The upside of the "unmet needs" conundrum is that research acknowledges that caregivers have them, too. Caregivers need education, resources, respite, and stress relief. When these needs are not met, all hell breaks loose. What I needed was someone else to deal with the little orphan girl my mom was reverting back to. Something in it was too painful for me, too close, or too provoking. Luckily for me, and doubly lucky for my mom, my husband was fairly immune to the triggers that drove me crazy. Where I lacked all capacity to cajole my way into giving care, my husband could cut through my mother's defenses and eventually make her laugh at her own preposterous claims. "No really, I can get myself home from the hospital on my own. You don't need to drive me." He could take it all in stride, but not all the time, naturally. The care team we had put in place was working well, but it still wasn't enough. To preserve our (remaining) sanity, I had to brush off my mantra and get back to work. Little orphan girl was going to need a whole lot more man hours.

12. THE A-TEAM

At the beginning of every new quarter in my yoga classes, I ask students to share some of their goals or successes. I am always happy to have new students who want to get in shape or learn how to relax, but it's especially gratifying to see the same people come back quarter after quarter, reaping so many benefits from their practice. And when they share their brief stories of healing and strength and greater tolerance with the new students, they make my job of retaining the new ones that much easier. One woman who always came straight from work, a little late and harried looking, had a great number of physical issues. She could not do all the gentle poses we did in the class, but she did what she could and she came back year after year. One time, during this beginning-of-the-quarter introduction period, she shared that her life was incredibly stressful because of demands of work, a sick husband, and her own failing health. She said that she'd find herself saying, "I can't do all this! I just can't do it." But then, as if from an eagle's vantage, she realized that even as she was telling herself that she couldn't do it, she actually was doing it. She didn't apply a pop psychology "be positive" approach; she said that she just had

116

those moments of grace in which she saw things as they really were.

When I had glimpses of how things really were, primarily that there were real dangers we needed to avoid and that my mother had greater needs than I could handle, I'd go back to my quest for better, more, or simply different kinds of care to give my mother. Even before the second incident of wandering and my subsequent takeover of the checkbook, my mom had caregivers coming Monday, Wednesday, and Friday for two-hour visits. After I took control of the checkbook, when future wandering seemed like a grim possibility, I looked for more care and took a different route. Instead of going through an agency, I got the name of a woman who had graduated from support group after her mother died, who also happened to take yoga classes with a teacher I knew. It seemed like a winning combination. More importantly, she had time in her schedule and was willing to give it a go.

There are many arguments against finding caregivers "under the radar," as some might say. Who is vetting them, for instance, and what about employee taxes and social security? What happens when they get sick and can't come? What about insurance if the caregiver falls when she's in your mom's house? All of these might be concerns great enough to keep you from asking around at support group for names of folks you might hire. And yet. Through word of mouth, and then an interview, and a check of their references, you might just find someone who's a perfect fit. With an agency, you get a case manager who can find someone who'll work with your schedule, but you might not meet all those agency employees and have no way of knowing what they're like unless you have time to attend both the intake interview and the first visit. Agencies will try to sell you on the safety and reliability of their services, and that's understandable; they definitely serve an important and necessary function in our community.

The woman I hired through word-of-mouth references had a flexible approach that I had not seen in agency caregivers. And because she had been a caregiver for her own mother and knew this rocky path, she brought ideas to the table that others might have been educated on but hadn't needed to apply. Closer in age to my mom than me, she could possibly play the part of a friend, though neither of us could pull off introducing the new arrangement as anything other than what it was: a new person to spend time with my mom.

Getting a new caregiver in the door was always a hassle. Case manager visits, interviews, fake smiles. With Julia, on the other hand, I replaced the awkward living-room interview by announcing, "Julia's going to walk with us today!" and we got in the car and went. Julia got to observe how I interacted with my mother in this more "natural" environment, and she could use that information to shape her own interactions with my mother. She insisted, in their relationship, on giving my mother choices—like where to walk, or which shop to visit—which first seemed unnecessary and possibly confusing to my mother, but I saw that her gentle way, much gentler than my dictatorial, "Okay, get your shoes on!" built trust. And for me, things seemed so much simpler and more fluid with Julia. I could ask her to take my mom to the store and she would either use one of my mom's checks that I'd mail her, or she'd pay herself and be reimbursed later. She'd see that the trash can needed emptying and help my mom do it. She'd let me know if the downstairs bathroom ran out of toilet paper. She'd see that my mom dressed appropriately for the weather. And she emailed me regular updates. This is not to say an agency caregiver couldn't do all these things, but none, in my experience to that point, ever had. None had come close to delivering that level of care without me having to ask for it specifically. Julia took initiative and met needs I didn't even know my mom or I had.

For instance, about six months into the job Julia came up with the brilliant idea of getting my mom trained as a Humane

Society volunteer. With nothing more than a few emails to confirm that it was okay with me, she got the whole thing set up: application, training, buying the volunteer t-shirt, and getting the shift onto my mom's schedule. Every Monday from 1:30-3 my mom now had a "job" of going to the Humane Society with Julia and petting lonely cats, a job that clearly addressed a need for meaningful engagement. Julia's other weekly outing with my mom always had them taking long and interesting walks on the many trails around Bellingham. A six mile walk on the north shore of Lake Whatcom, the railroad trail from Scudder Pond to Barkley Village, Squires Lake, the Boulevard Trail, and on and on. On each outing Julia gave my mom time and space to greet babies, pet dogs, and, presumably, pick up rocks, her new and growing obsession.

Building on the success of finding Julia outside of an agency, I thought I could find more help by placing an ad myself and finding the next Nanny McPhee-like magician on my own. I posted a notice on the local student job board and got about 10 replies, all very positive and enthusiastic, then set about the less enjoyable task of arranging interviews. The candidates had helped with their grandma or they were taking psychology classes. They had volunteered in a nursing home or they hoped to go into medicine. They all looked very promising on paper, but in the flesh, they were simply too young. They didn't have cars—a requirement I forgot to put in the ad—and they didn't seem to know how to initiate conversation, even with me. If I was making them nervous, think how they'd respond the first time my mom met them at the door in her bathrobe and told them with a scowl that she didn't need their help. How would they have the confidence to get past that? How would they find the chutzpah to barge in and, at a minimum, find and administer her morning meds? At a maximum, stall for time till she forgot her resistance then get her dressed and out the door for a walk? No, I couldn't see it.

One of them, however, an older-than-average college student returning for a degree in environmental studies, had some possibilities. She was a non-stop talker, unlike the shy younger students I'd been interviewing, and a little eccentric, but she had experience working with an older man with Alzheimer's and she came with a strong reference. Plus, it turned out she lived just a block from my mother so could help out with odd half-hour shifts, if need be, or longer morning or afternoon spots as her school schedule allowed. I thought, okay, viva la difference, so what if she has a little conspiracy theory bent and can't keep her opinions to herself? It'll keep my mother engaged.

We met at my mom's house a week later for our walking interview. I knew my mother was always resistant and could never remember that some of these "visitors" actually contributed greatly to her life, so I was ready for that. But her resistance to this woman, with her nonstop talking and conversational detours into the Mayan calendar and faith healing, along with zealous trail maintenance that had her picking up any scrap of litter she saw along the way, disclaiming on its dangers to animals, biodegradability, etc., while her arms were getting fuller and fuller, verged on the comical.

Halfway through the walk my mother stopped talking entirely. At one point, with a look of abject terror on her face, she asked me in a whisper, "She's not coming over to walk with me, is she?" No. However convenient it would have been for me and however eager this woman was, no. No way. Little orphan girl was finally speaking up for herself! Though I'd now spent several hours with this woman I wouldn't be hiring, I counted the experience a success nonetheless. I learned that I should have gone with my first instincts—crazy talk is crazy talk, even to a person with dementia—and I saw that my mom and I could still agree on a few fundamentals.

I gave up my search for more outside care after that experience and stuck with the routine we had. Then some months later, reenergized, I called a woman who'd been recommended by a friend of a friend. Completely different from the caregivers my mom had had before—closer to my age than my mom's, with gorgeous, long, dark, curly hair my mom would love, and into sewing and beading and other creative projects—she had a sparkle I admired because I lacked it entirely. I set up another walking interview, and it was a hit. My mom didn't telegraph any terror about Cynthia's personality, and Cynthia knew right where to go to appeal to my mom: right to her love of color, trinkets, and baubles. They were a match made in a glittery, handcrafted heaven. I added Cynthia to my mom's schedule, bringing it up to four caregiving sessions per week.

At around this point my husband, too, got on board as a regular visitor. He had been helpful before—listening to me complain, mostly—by spending many hours looking for my mom's purse, helping with household maintenance, or taking her dog to the vet. Being on the weekly schedule required a much greater commitment. Getting him to agree required nothing more than my asking, but as everyone who cares for someone knows, asking isn't always easy. It takes you to a vulnerable place where guilt, need, and fear live, a place it's easier to lock up tight with a chain and a padlock than have to enter. But I did it, and he said yes.

Paul's shift, another two days a week, involved crossword puzzles. With credible research on my side, I have strongly and resoundingly rejected the popular claim advice givers make that crossword puzzles, Sudoku, or anagrams will "keep you from getting Alzheimer's." No, I routinely say, doing crossword puzzles will not prevent you from getting Alzheimer's; it will simply make you better at doing crossword puzzles. But after seeing Paul work with my mother through many large print, easy puzzle books, I should change my response. Doing crosswords won't prevent dementia, but if you're good at coming up with analogies, enjoy charades, and are an A+ cajoler, it can be a pretty amusing way to spend your time with someone once they've got it.

Every visit started with some variation of, "Come on Pat, we're going to do a crossword puzzle," and was met with, "Oh Paul, you know I can't do those things." And then they'd be off. She did best with fill-in-the blank answers, where the expression is a familiar phrase. "Here today, __ tomorrow." "Gone," she'd say, and Paul would respond, "See, there's another one you got right; you're doing the whole thing." She would probably not understand exactly what might be "thrown into the ring," but if Paul hammed it up a bit and said, "Pat, I'm throwing my __ into the ring," maybe making a tossing gesture, emphasizing the blank with raised eyebrows, and pantomiming a hat, she would get it. A good 80% of the time she'd say, "I have no idea," or, when she heard the answer, "I never heard that word before." Parka, ilk, reeks, pompous, luau. All gone. But say "Bing," and she'd be sure to get "Crosby." Do crosswords meet the very desperate need of disease prevention? Surely not. But they did, undeniably, address my mother's need for companionship, humor, male attention in a sea of female faces, and gentle mental stimulation. The crosswords were gentle attempts to keep restretching the canvas that wanted to curl in on itself. "Peek-__, I see you!" was just a few centimeters beyond "Bah Bah __ Sheep," which was a welcome respite from her standard repertoire which she inevitably found her way back to. "Paul, have you heard from your father?" "What grade is Wilson in again?" and a perennial favorite: "I never see Denise anymore."

Was it true? Was I so successful in lining up outside care for my mother that I never saw her myself? No, but I wasn't done yet, either. I had yet to talk my mom into the best source of outside care our community had to offer, but I was close.

The program, called Adult Day Health, provides lunch, mental stimulation, physical therapy, social interactions, and fun. I knew about ADH from the very beginning of my mother's journey into Alzheimer's, but in the earliest stages she was nowhere near ready for it. A couple years into the progression, when we did come in to talk with one of the in-take nurses and see the program in action, my mother gave her classic whole-body shudder, clamped her lips together in a frown, and said what every old person says at some time or another: "I don't want to spend time with all of those old people." A year later we tried again and she had the same reaction. She looked stricken, desolate, like a child you could absolutely not leave at kindergarten no matter how many other mothers had left their children screaming at the gate before you.

From the vantage of cognitive and physical health, the land of freedom to do as you please, where you can stream a movie from Netflix or drive to the store for a bottle of wine, the landscape of a highly orchestrated, tightly controlled Adult Day Health program can look hellishly confining. That's how my mom saw it initially, and then one day, it didn't look so bad. We showed up one morning and she saw that hey, it's actually kind of fun to sit in a circle with other old folks and toss a bean bag through a hole cut into a board. Or sing songs. Or play simple games that ask you to reflect on your favorite, or only, memories. My mother, who was prone to patting gray-haired ladies on the shoulder, cooing at people in wheelchairs, and saying "bless their soul" when she saw anyone over 60 crossing the street unassisted, ate it up. Not only could she pat away to her heart's content, but she was going to get her share of patting and cooing in return.

With this last piece of the caregiving puzzle in place, I started to feel that I was beginning to meet my mother's need for attention and care, and I was doing it while honoring her determined wish to stay in her own home. Placing her into any other living arrangement still seemed as out of the question as it ever had, but now, at least, I felt comfortable knowing that she spent fewer hours alone. Nothing on the dementia journey is ever really "solved," but as an email to a friend from that time shows, I had reached a new plateau. "I am basking in the illusory glow of having fixed something for my mom," I wrote. "I feel like we are at a stable place right now, like I got something right. But I know that this will not last. A time will come and something will have to happen, and it will be back to 'what is least terrible?'" For the time being, there was nothing terrible that needed fixing. Every day was manageable. I was still in charge, but now I had so many others to help.

With that little bit of mental and emotional space, I could ease up a bit, relax. I could, but what I did instead was dive headlong into planning another trip, this one longer and more complicated than any we'd done before. We'd spend two weeks "wwoofing"—working on farms in England and Scotland for room and board—we'd see plays, take a 5-day bike ride along the British coast, stay in a camper van on the Isle of Mull, hike hills and coasts from Skye to Solva, go to museums, and hear music. It is ironic that I found enjoyment here, given the great number of unknowns and then-whats involved in trip planning. You'd think I had enough problem-solving challenges in caring for my mother. But in coming back to my computer and my guidebooks over and over in this new frenzy of planning, I had tapped into one of those "unmet needs." Our son was 15 and just about to the expiry date for enjoying, or even tolerating, 24/7 companionship with his parents. If all went well, he'd go to college in a few years and we'd be on our own. So trip planning, with all its repetitive or maybe downright compulsive acts of reading, searching, checking, and deciding, gave me the paradoxical pleasures of looking forward and holding on. The trip would take me out of caregiving all together for a full six weeks, and it would give me the same amount of time to savor what would, in the natural course of things, be coming to an end.

13. RENEWED

"Are you okay with bringing beer?"

Getting everything in place for our six-week trip included creating elaborate Excel files to account for all the necessary comings and goings to my mom's house and hiring one more caregiver. Since you really have no idea what belief systems you're going to run up against when you hire strangers, it's good to ask the delicate questions up front. "Are you okay driving around with a case of beer in your trunk so that you have them with you when you do your shift?" It would have been nicer if the beer could be delivered cold, but I couldn't push it. Another criteria for the new caregiver was dog care. Could they give my mom's dog her eye drops? I wanted to think that anyone trained to toilet and bathe a dependent senior would be fine with a sick dog, but I also thought it safe to have them meet the dog first.

"Where's Doozy?" was still a frequent question, but Doozy was never very far. Usually she could be found making tight circular loops in the kitchen or living room, sometimes out on the lawn. Her days of running away were long gone. A combination of unfortunate health issues had left Doozy with kidney damage, high blood pressure, infected gums, poor bladder control, and near blindness. She was receiving meds for all of these, but nothing was likely to cure her. She was about 12 years old and had lost 4 of her original 12 pounds in the last half year. It had become a waiting game. But waiting for what? My mother would say, "I hope Doozy and I can go together," and "I don't know how I'll live when I don't have Doozy." While I didn't really anticipate her accompanying Doozy to the grave, I didn't want to take any chances. But wasn't it all a big chance? Sick dog or not, was I insane for thinking I could leave my mother for six weeks?

The 36-Hour Day includes this interesting observation on respite care: "Some caregivers are reluctant to use short-stay respite; they fear that once they give up the burden of care, even temporarily, they will be unable to shoulder it again" (313). "Unable" is a strong word in that sentence and hit me like a bolt of lightning. Unable? What if I didn't go back to caregiving after my break? What then? Those cases must exist, but I don't hear about them at support group because we're all there, shoulder to the wheel, doing the best we can, learning as we go. Aside from those whose parents have died, only a very few people who've attended support group over the years have arrived at a juncture where the caregiving burden is permanently lifted from them. In the three cases I've seen, the parent moved to another location to be closer to other siblings. In one of those cases, the mom moved, stayed a while, then got sent back. Tag, you're it again.

It does not seem to be the case for most of the people I've met over the years at support group that they are unable to shoulder the burden. It seems, in more cases than not, that they don't see any way not to. Some will even say that caregiving for a parent becomes their life's privilege and blessing, but I am unable to go that far. On my best days I can laugh and have a good time with my mother and live in platitudes like, "It is what it is" and not get too bogged down. On my average days I live another cliché: "Keep calm and carry on." And when things are getting a little dicey and I need to stay focused, I recall yet another cliché offered up by a caregiver who spoke to us on the importance of maintaining a sense of humor: "Git 'er done." Clichés, mantras, meditation, yoga, a walk in the woods, a cuddle with my dog . . . I use whatever I can.

If it were as simple as "git 'er done," however, there wouldn't be so many books and conferences and articles encouraging caregivers to take care of themselves. If it were instinctual to balance the work of caregiving with necessary breaks as soon as your nerves start to feel fried, we wouldn't have research showing that caregivers are more likely to suffer depression and stress related diseases than the average non-caregiving person. I believe that what keeps us locked into the most stressful aspects of caregiving and keeps us from waving our white flags of surrender is a secret fear that one, it won't help—we may rest up and start to feel good again, but then we'll be right back in it, so why bother—and two, however unhappy it makes us, we believe we're irreplaceable. Or maybe the block is much more straightforward: it takes a lot of time and careful planning to make an escape possible. It's one thing to have a schedule in place for daily visits, food preparation, meds, walks, dog duty, etc. when you live down the street and can be called in if something goes wrong. It's another thing all together to hire someone to do all that and then leave.

Of course guilt plays a large part in it ("I shouldn't be going off and having a good time"), along with shame ("What's wrong with me that I think of caregiving a burden anyway?"), and whatever else you bring into the relationship from your whole life preceding the diagnosis. It didn't help, either, that leading up to our trip I felt like a pretender at support group. Here were the true caregivers: dedicated daughters and sons seeing to their parent's issues on a constant, unrelenting basis. Some parents were finally making the move from their family home to assisted living. Some were in and out of the hospital. One man reported that his mother cried most of the day. One woman told how her father had decided that if he converted a drill into a sander, maybe he could vibrate the dementia right out of his wife's brain. And he wasn't even the parent the daughter was worried about! These were children who deserved to be called caregivers. I was the daughter who didn't even own a cell phone who was now leaving the country for six weeks. Seeing through the layers of my conflicted feelings, our support group leader was completely behind my ambitious plan. Go, she said, and have a great time. And, despite all my concerns, I did. Out of the 42 days we were gone, on only one or two of them did I receive slightly alarming emails from the sister-in-law I'd left in charge. One day I had mis-scheduled the delivery of my mom's medications and heard about the scuffle that ensued; another email reported a decision someone made to take Doozy to the vet. Apart from those concerns and a few other incidents my kind sister-in-law didn't share with me, nothing happened. The sky did not fall. Care was given; care was received. We made our escape and my mother survived.

After the trip I heard from my neighbor that my mother had been over to our house regularly, poking around in my garden, watering, maybe doing a little trimming. She'd carried her dog with her on at least one occasion, then went home without it, then later came back looking for it, assuring my neighbor that no, no, everything was fine, but had they seen a little white dog by any chance? These were the kinds of incidents no one emailed me about while we were gone, the kind I only found out about by chance. As when another neighbor a few blocks down told me she had seen my mom walking to the store with her pink cart. This was a full year after I took over the checkbook, so my mom, on her own, had no way to buy groceries. "You mean you saw her last year?" I asked, confused. "No," she said, "yesterday." One day home from my six-week respite and I was right back in it, right back down the rabbit hole.

Getting back into the rhythm of caregiving was made more interesting by the fact that my son and husband were heading out on a two-week river trip just two days after we returned. So after 24/7 companionship for six solid weeks, I would be left on my own. I'd have my shifts with my mom as well as Paul's shifts, but still plenty of time by myself for yoga, walking the dog, and catching up with friends. It would have been perfect if it hadn't been for the mice.

Mice had made their way into our house during our absence, leaving turds and even one corpse in an old trap we'd left under the kitchen sink from an earlier incursion. And as if those weren't bad enough, my son saw a live one in his bedroom. We had no time for jet lag. My son and I tackled the mess he'd left in his room those six weeks, I cleaned out all the kitchen cupboards, and my husband set traps everywhere. For the two days before he departed, he emptied them of fresh corpses twice a day. Then my two helpers took off, leaving me alone with the mice. And my mother. Who apparently has no fear whatsoever.

For the two weeks that my husband was away I had my mother over every day to help me check traps. I'd hold the flashlight and she'd hold a plastic bag and tongs. I'd swing the cupboard door open and jump five feet backward while she stood there squinting into the darkness. On two occasions, when the mice were just caught by a foot and were still alive, scraping around in the cupboard, I'd scream, and she'd say, "Stop that. You're making me nervous." I tried to obey her, my new savior.

Had my 6-week break from my mother given me a new perspective? A new way to appreciate her? Or was it simply that anyone would be grateful for their 76-year-old mother's willingness to reach into a dark cupboard and pull out a trap with a still-warm corpse in it? My next visit to support group had me telling this delightful my-mother-my-hero story—and while it probably wasn't the first time I related events that weren't tinged with a little self-pity and pain—I do think it marked a turning point. Had I ever, in all my years of going to support group, said that my mother was actually helping me?

Mouse hunter, laundry folder, flower arranger, bauble collector. My mother still had so many strengths. She still exercised skills and talents I'd never had, and she seemed to be getting easier. Had my respite from caregiving given me new eyes with which to see her? Maybe, but it was also clear that her confusion was increasing. She started to call my son her nephew and would offer gifts to him more suited to a four- or five-year old. She'd say, "How's your husband?" instead of using Paul's name. How soon, I wondered, before she forgot who he was. Or forgot me. Could she still live on her own when everyone in her life became a stranger? She was already past the point of remembering any of her caregivers. Even within an hour of coming home from one of her outings she'd say thoughtfully, "I'm a little bored because I've been sitting here at home all day." But she recognized all her caregivers when they arrived, let them in, and went off on grand adventures nearly every day of the week.

At support group our leader tells new arrivals who are desperate for answers, "Everyone does things differently." She'll say, "There's a lot of wisdom in the group," but she makes clear that each of our situations is unique. None of us can provide a failsafe formula for dealing with a parent with dementia, and it's through the variety of approaches and stories that we learn and grow. The process necessarily matures us, and it appears that those who only want to use group as a platform to complain, or give unwanted advice, or ask questions that could be answered by a simple Google search, don't come back. The woman who showed up one night and asked, "Why does my mother say such stupid things?" probably wasn't satisfied with the level and tenor of our discussion. We weren't there to call our parents stupid and make ourselves feel better by disrespecting them, though we were all quite willing to laugh at situations that were often as tragic as they were comical.

People offended by our levity probably don't come back, either, and I often wonder what becomes of them. I wonder if they have enough support outside group, or if they're just too worn out to come. I have to guard against telling the weary-looking ones that what they really need is to take a trip, to get out of there, even if for the weekend, to trust the care of their loved one to someone else for a while. It worked for me, I know, but it's not for me to tell others how to carry on. Still, I know for myself that getting away is the only way to stay in it for the long haul, just like coming to support group is a necessary monthly release. It's such a crazy, up-and-down, bumpy ride. Why travel it alone if you don't have to? Why not step off the path for a short time and see if, upon your return, you find something new?

14. SECRET LIVES

If my six-week trip changed my perspective and helped me appreciate what my mother still had to share with me, it also changed her routine in a lasting way. I took back my shifts and put my husband back into the rotation, but I didn't decrease the hours of care my mom received to pre-trip levels. I saw with appreciation that her full roster of caregivers offered a nice variety of company, excursions, and stimulation. Plus, Doozy was in serious decline.

During the three weeks we'd been home, there'd been many more trips to the vet, two- or three-times-a-day administration of pills and eye drops, and frequent cleaning of dog messes found around the house and on the bottom of my mother's shoes. And the situation required lots of consoling. My mother's anticipatory grief did not have so far to travel now, as death was clearly on its way. One look at Doozy—blind, thin, walking in circles, often knocking into cupboards and walls—and you knew her time was near and might wonder if it was still humane to keep her alive. Then one afternoon when I was out, one of the caregivers called to say that Doozy was seizing. My mom was holding her, but nothing seemed to help. She was urinating; she was vomiting. Systems were failing. Even my mom, who found much to cherish in this dog that had become more sorrow than solace, knew it was time.

I wasn't there and couldn't be reached because, I think I have confessed, I do not own a cell phone. But Paul, my proxy, did everything I would have done. He called the vet and explained what was happening then, taking our son with him, went to my mom's and gathered her and Doozy into the car for their last trip together. Past the park we always went to when Doozy could still walk, past the cemetery, into the vet's office where my mom would say goodbye to the third and final dog she'd ever have to put down. Remarkably, she wasn't crushed. The woman who'd said she wanted to die when Doozy died, or, failing that, would move into "a home" when she didn't have her little friend anymore, got back into the car and, with Doozy's body in a box on her lap, sat quietly for the ride home. The somber trio stopped to get me, knowing I'd be home from my outings by then. I'd read the oddly formal note left for me on the white board: "Made a 5:15 appointment at the vet to euthanize Doozy," so I was ready when my son called up from the garage, "Come on. We're going to bury Doozy."

In my mom's backyard, Paul dug a hole between two young but well established trees, hitting roots not more than 18-inches down. Realizing it wasn't the time to play supervisor, and not having the proper footwear or determination to dig a deeper hole myself, I suggested that we at least cover the cardboard coffin with as much loose dirt as we could and mark the spot with something heavy. An ornamental owl sculpture was at hand, so we set it atop the small mound, looked sadly at each other, then went inside where it now seemed much quieter. My mom had laundered the sheets that Doozy had soiled the night before, their last night together, so we helped her make her bed, tried to get her to eat some dinner, and offered another round of condolences. Now we were the ones repeating ourselves.

As we got ready to leave, it struck me that she'd be alone now. It wasn't like Doozy had provided care or security, but without her there, I feared that my mom would lose her will to live and make good on her desire that they "go together." I also worried that she'd start each day looking for Doozy, not remembering that she was dead. But for a few days she did remember, and remembering made her sad, and her sadness was simple. It had nothing to do with Alzheimer's and everything to do with the normal human emotions surrounding loss.

But then, within a week of Doozy's death, the grave marker, the 20-pound owl with a bobbing head and unnaturally alert amber eyes, was moved onto my mom's kitchen counter. Casually, not using the words "Doozy" or "grave," I asked why it was there, what had made her bring it in from outside. "Oh, I just like it," she said. Later it appeared on a table in her living room, and then it got put into the rotating circuit of plants and rocks and baubles that filled her house. And with that, there was no more talk of Doozy. The friends she used to keep in touch with, her son, some beloved nieces and nephews, most of her memories, and now Doozy. All forgotten. Then, at the suggestion of Katie, one of her caregivers, she got a cat.

One of my steadfast rules about caregivers is that they must reduce the burden, not add to it. If a caregiver requires me to spend more time dealing with my mother, whether because the caregiver increases my mother's anxiety, needs extensive handholding, loses my mother's keys, loses her own keys at my mother's house, etc., then it's really not worth it. Conducting a simple cost-benefit analysis, I weigh the price of what we're paying out against the peace of mind we're getting in return. Hiring the crazy talker who made my mom flinch wouldn't have been worth it at any price, whereas the community relations director of a nearby facility who'd show up occasionally for no charge whatsoever, usually with a plate of cookies, was a definite keeper. What I discovered, too, is that I didn't have to even really like the caregiver as long as she did her job; it was the relationship between my mom and the caregiver that mattered most. Expecting that the caregiver be someone I'd enjoy spending time with was probably asking too much.

Pema Chodron has a lovely way of discussing what happens to us when we're "bugged." She talks about how we all have triggers—those little things that irritate us or "hook" us into extremely uncomfortable feelings that make us want to flee, fight back, or scream. She says that like bug bites, which trigger a reflexive response to scratch, which in turn gives temporary relief but makes the initial insult to our skin even worse, these hooks bring up old patterns of behavior that perpetuate rather than ameliorate our suffering. All to say, some caregivers will get under your skin, and you'll have to decide if it's worth scratching or if it's better to try to breathe and let go.

Katie pushed buttons in me that had to do with knowledge and competence—what I knew about Alzheimer's and what I was doing for my mother's care—two areas of inquiry where I felt I'd been pretty diligent. Whenever we spoke, I felt bulldozed by her projections and assumptions. I'd listen as politely as I could and try to steer the conversation back to safe employer-employee territory: did she have what she needed to do her job, was it working out? The relationship she had with my mom was going well, I thought, so with great effort I tried to stop scratching the itch. And then, just when I'd regained a more composed outlook, she asked me if my mom could take Buddy.

Buddy was a stray tabby who'd been loitering behind Katie's house. Katie had taken my mother there to do simple, around-the-house projects, and on several of those occasions my mother got to meet this friendly stray. Not wanting the cat herself, Katie had been trying to place him, and following Doozy's death, asked my mother what she thought about having a cat. To her credit, she also asked me, and I made my position clear: if it made more work for me, then no. We had just

135

been through elaborate and painful proxy dog care, and I wasn't interested in starting all over again with a stray cat. Katie assured me that if the cat became a problem, she'd take it back.

I have already discussed the short shelf life of explanatory notes and reminders for a person with Alzheimer's. The sign you hang over the hook that says, "Put your keys here" would likely get found a week later with the missing keys. The reminder, "Denise has your purse and will take you shopping" wouldn't work because the first time my mom read it she'd think, "I don't need that," and would call me to ask to get her purse back. But for all she claimed to know about Alzheimer's care and was over eager to share with me, Katie didn't seem to know about the uselessness of these kinds of explanations. When she showed up with Buddy, she brought six pages of handwritten instructions for my mom to follow. Number one was to keep the cat in the garage for two days, along with the litter box, so the cat could learn where to do its business. The next step was to keep the cat inside another week or so, until it felt comfortable, and then there were instructions about taking it to the vet, brushing it, which cat food to get, the importance of a collar, and so on. Within the first few hours, the cat was outside. My mom had opened the door to the garage and been surprised to see a cat in there, so she let it out. Thinking that she'd stumbled upon a stray, she wondered what she should do to find the cat's owner. Should she put up a sign?

More notes from Katie appeared over the next few weeks, like, "Feed the cat kibble." Good luck with that, I'd think, as I threw away the desiccated enchilada my mom had put down for the cat's dinner. Notes like, "Buddy should wear his collar since he goes outside," that I'd find folded up in the drawer where you could find everything from empty raisin boxes to burned out light bulbs to brand new, unused cat collars. Then Katie suggested we take the cat in for a wellness exam and get a microchip put in. Rolling my eyes as far up into my skull as I possibly could without tearing a muscle, I told Katie, "I'll leave a check. You can make an appointment and take my mom and the cat during your next shift."

When you delegate, you buy yourself time or freedom. The downside is that you're not there to see for yourself, so you have to rely on others to tell you what happened. When your mother with Alzheimer's is your chief informant, you get a slightly wonky version of what you missed, or possibly no version at all. Katie filled me in on the facts: it turned out that the cat already had a microchip, but the chip had no information attached to it. A dead end. All we learned was that the chip was ten years old and inserted by a vet about 30 miles away. But for all that, the experiment seemed to be working. Buddy stayed with my mom and my mom enjoyed his company. The only wrinkle in this happy new development was the appearance of the mean lady.

A confabulation most likely born out of confusion over the cat's ownership, the mean lady became a staple in every conversation I had with my mother for the next year. The mean lady, or sometimes just "that woman," would show up on my mom's doorstep, demanding that my mother give the cat back. Sometimes she phoned. From my mother's telling, which was delivered with nearly the same words every time, "the woman was not very happy." The first few times I heard this, I worried. Who had been over at my mom's asking for the cat? Why had the vet, or Katie, given anyone her phone number? Then I saw it: the trip to the vet's and the microchip incident had morphed into a fear that a rightful owner would show up to claim the cat.

The story had to be my mom's way of making sense of a cat that kept appearing and disappearing from her life every time she opened the door and let it out, and every time she opened the door and let it back in. Sometimes the cat didn't even have to be outside to be gone. The cat might be sitting quietly on a table in the living room and my mom would launch into the story. It wasn't a case of "out of sight, out of mind," but something more like, "Out of sight? Well, it's because of that mean lady."

At first I tried to reorient my mom to recent history—remember how the cat used to live at Katie's, and then came here? Remember how there was no owner information associated with the chip?—but that was no better than a six-page note. I decided to just go with it, and in hearing the story over and over, began to detect a whiff of the orphan girl. I heard again the old hurts dispensed by the various "mean" ladies in my mom's fragmented memories, including the babysitters who'd locked her and her brother outside all day. This new mean lady was more aggressive, though, and angry. My mom had something she wanted. At times the story took new twists, like how the cat escaped from her fully enclosed garage, or how she found out where the mean lady lived, but mostly it stayed the same and explained Buddy's comings and goings perfectly well.

And then a new thing emerged. In the telling, my mom started displaying a bit of an attitude, like she was ready for a fight. "Well," she'd say, "unless that woman keeps him locked inside, I can't stop him from coming back here when he wants to." "He must like you better," I'd encourage, "You've given him a nice home." Too modest to agree outright, but agreeing all the same, she'd go on, "If that woman comes over and tells me she wants him back, I'll just say he likes coming over here now." By that point she'd be jutting her chin forward slightly, like a fighter not afraid to take a hit. Who was closing the door in someone else's face now? The little orphan girl emerged victorious.

I grew to appreciate the cat, despite the new story it gave rise to and its million retellings, but I had to wonder: did it do anything to help fill the many hours my mom still spent alone every day? I knew that Doozy had given my mom's day some structure, back when Doozy could still take walks with her, anyway, but what did the cat do? In these post-dog days I found myself wondering, again, on my mom's behalf, what the right balance was between company and solitude, between taking responsibility for another creature's life and receiving care for her own.

I also wondered about, and even suggested, the possibility of a roommate. On one hand, my mother found the idea of having someone live with her quite compelling. She'd have company. She'd have someone to do things with. On the other hand, it activated her aversions: the person would have to clean up after herself, and be quiet, and cook her own food, and not bring friends over, and so on. In this way, she was no different than any of us, imagining a best of all possible worlds scenario that's unlikely to ever come true. When we veered toward the topic of her moving to "a place," the pros and cons were meted out similarly: yes, there'd be someone to talk to, but that would be a con as much as a pro. All those people to talk to, day and night, at every meal, any time you left your private domain. Though my mom can be the friendliest person in the room, warm, considerate, and shoulder patting, she can also be as belligerent as Gold Hat in the film version of *The Treasure of the Sierra Madre*. "Badges? We ain't got no badges.... I don't have to show you any stinkin' badges!"

The question constantly circled back to safety: Was it still safe for her to live alone? And the question of safety pivoted on tolerance. How safe? What is an acceptable risk to safety ratio? As Atul Gawande notes in his discussion of the original concept behind assisted living facilities in his book *Being Mortal,* there isn't a simple answer. He asks, "Is someone who refuses regular housekeeping, smokes cigarettes, and eats candies that cause a diabetic crisis requiring a trip to the hospital someone who is a victim of neglect or an archetype of freedom?" (92). My question about my mom went something like this: Was I maintaining the status quo because it honored her stated wish to live at home, or was I simply too cowardly to take the necessary next step? Because a dementia diagnosis puts an expiry date on one's "freedom to choose," was I being irresponsible in not choosing for her?

But then I had to remind myself: I had chosen. I'd chosen to keep her at home as long as I possibly could, to stay in the present moment as much as possible, and to not, even at what looked like the middle stage of the disease, over-catastrophize. Call it the negative space plan. I could focus not so much on the central subject of the picture—my mom, living alone with progressive memory loss—but on everything that continued to fill the space around her.

Like Buddy. One evening when I went over to visit, I found my mom already in bed. I sat in the rocking chair near her and took Buddy onto my lap. He took a few pets from me then walked across my legs to the bed and stretched himself out across my mother's torso. He extended his two front legs up past her collar bones, resting one paw on each side of her neck. "This is how we snuggle," she said, looking childlike and delighted, and I couldn't wish anything sweeter for my mom than that cat's warm embrace. A few moments later she added reflectively, "Sometimes, though he doesn't mean to, he opens his claws and makes a little scratch on my neck." Love and pain, snuggles and scratches. Was there any other way?

Buddy's comings and goings and his supposed secret life with that "other woman" provided me a new way to look at my mother's life. Sometimes I was with her, so I knew where she was. Sometimes I shared meals with her, so I knew what she ate. Sometimes I took walks with her, so I knew where she had been. But when I wasn't there, I had no idea what she was doing. Even with notes from her caregivers to fill me in, I saw her life as if shrouded in mystery. At times she seemed no more familiar to me than a character in someone else's novel: "Pat was standing at the door when I got there," or "Pat was upstairs, still in her pajamas." "We had a good time poking around Joe's Garden," or "Your mom helped me fold clothes."

"We took a long walk along the Boulevard and had hot chocolate," or "We went out to Boomer's and your mom had a whole bacon cheeseburger and fries." Without the notes I would be clueless because if I asked her how her day was, a question that hadn't really been useful for a couple of years, or tried to prompt her to find out what she did on her outings, I got nothing. "No, I haven't been out," she'd say, or she'd ask, "Did I go somewhere today? I don't think so. I don't remember."

Just when I felt on the verge of sinking into guilt about all the hours I didn't spend with my mom—guilt and sadness that neither of us really knew what she thought or felt about any of her activities—I would try to think not of the central figures: me caring for my mom and my mom receiving care from me, but of all the supporting actors and props that made my mom's life enjoyable in the moment. I thought of Buddy the cat, that archetype of freedom, and the richness of his secret life. And I thought how, because she couldn't remember much at all about her own comings and goings, my mom had a secret life, too.

15. TREASURE

Five years after my mom received her Alzheimer's diagnosis, I found myself without a lot to say at support group. I observed that I was more likely to sit back and listen than present any new hair-pulling challenges. My mother had become, in my mind, the living proof of the claim that things got easier when they got worse because, despite all the losses and all the hard choices we'd made in the last couple years, there we were, apparently established in a reliable, satisfying routine. It might have been a bad omen to say it out loud, but I did anyway at the beginning of many meetings when we went around and introduced ourselves and said a little bit about the person we cared for: my mom seemed happy. Happy, healthy, and still walking. Often alone. As long as she made it home on her own steam I didn't want to call it "wandering," but saying simply that my mom "took a walk" every day, and not admitting how crazy making it could be, wasn't accurate, either.

When I did raise the subject in group or with anyone who ever asked how my mom was doing, I would stress the positive. Her physical health was amazing, and I knew that walking had, most assuredly, been a key factor in what appeared to be her remarkably slow decline. What I also knew to be true was that walking had become for my mother what hand washing is to some people with obsessive compulsive disorder. Not an option. And because of the dementia, the potency of her need to walk was matched only by her failure to recall that she already had. On our Sunday mornings together, for instance, we'd go to the park and walk for an hour or so, always a time and distance that made her happy to see the car waiting for us in the parking lot. Next we'd stop at the grocery store and then head back to her house. Before we made it into the driveway she'd already be asking me if I wanted to take a walk, like Groundhog Day on a treadmill. I might say we just had walked, or that I was tired, or I'd use some other method to try to distract her. It didn't matter. After I left she'd almost always head out on another walk, and I, by not joining her or finding yet more caregivers to occupy every hour of her day, implicitly gave her the green light to go.

But there was something else in it, something I might have shared at group in a gesture of "true confessions." I was still spending time with my mother and taking her on walks, but I was finding it increasingly difficult because of what appeared to be her new companion compulsion: a need to pick stuff up. A current favorite was white gravel. She still loved everything colorful and sparkly and wouldn't forgo bits of colored glass when they caught her eye, but at some point, white gravel had become an irresistible attractant. I began noticing that at the same exact place on our walk through the park, after we'd been around the cemetery then back to the off-leash area, my mom would inevitably fall a few steps behind me. When I looked back for her, she'd be bent over picking up a piece of gravel just a little bit whiter than the pieces next to it. The same patch of path, the same gravel, the same fascination each time. Isn't this pretty, she'd ask?

You might reasonably assume that at this point in my mom's Alzheimer's journey I'd have already spent down all of my impatience, but you'd be wrong.

For some reason, this new compulsion became a constant trigger. I tried ridiculous lines of argument with her, from pointing out that it was just gravel, that she might fall if she bent down too quickly or stood up too fast, or that she already had a bunch of gravel at home, each time berating myself later for denying her this simple pleasure and agreeing that yes, that particular piece of white gravel was amazing. Why couldn't I make that my mantra? Sensing my irritation, my mother would say, "You don't have to wait; I'll catch up," which left me feeling even more heartless as I'd find myself walking 20 paces ahead of her and then see her sweaty face as she trotted along to catch up. I'd console myself that the extra cardio was good for her and that she enjoyed looking for gravel more than she enjoyed my sourpuss company, and we'd continue our walk slightly apart—at least until the trail reentered the forest and the gravel path was behind us.

One day, not thinking about the force of gravel on my mother's imagination, I took her on a walk that began in a newly designed city park, wound its way up a hillside, and connected to an existing hike and bike trail that led to the beach. Too late, I looked ahead and realized my mistake. The entire trail had been freshly covered with white gravel. I played it cool and hoped she wouldn't notice, taking a quick look at what she was wearing to size up the carrying capacity of her pockets. I gave myself a pep talk, steeling myself for what was to come. It came quickly. Every tenth step or so she'd fall behind to satisfy her deep urge, each time chirping, "Don't stop. I'll catch up!" For the sheer physical relief of it, I'd roll my eyes fully around their sockets and stand there, waiting. And then, as if transported from Dante's 9th ring of hell to that scene in Contact when Jodie Foster gets to talk to her dad and glimpses the magnitude of our human potential, I got in front of my impatience and tried a new tack.

"Why do you like white gravel so much?" I asked. "I don't know," she said. Could it be that easy? Could we really just discuss it? She told me that she liked it, that it was pretty, and that she liked doing things with it. All of that was true. At home she had filled vases with it, arranged it on paper plates with pine cones and feathers, even made intricately patterned displays, alternating white gravel with darker rocks in a parfait-like arrangement. Seeing that she had already picked up a few handfuls, I asked her if she thought she had enough, if she could just walk with me and stop looking at the ground. That seemed wildly improbable, but I was feeling hopeful, and I also enjoyed actually talking to her and getting answers, not just repeating the same words from our familiar conversations. And for a moment, I was rewarded. Quietly reflective, she said, "I don't know. Something in my brain tells me it wants white gravel, and it's very hard for me to resist." I had rarely heard her be so thoughtful about her situation, so metacognitive. It made me wonder: With whom was I now speaking? Who gave the orders in there, and who obeyed? Encouraged, thinking I might be able to dethrone the gravel despot in my mom's head, I suggested, "What if we talk about something else, like when you got married, or how you met Dick, and see if that distracts you from the gravel for a while?" With childlike honesty she said, "Okay, but I don't think it will work." She was right. She got through the part in the story where she was working as a lifeguard at the kiddy pool—because she couldn't swim—and how she saw my dad and his friends looking at her, and how later they started dating, and . . . then another piece of gravel caught her attention and her earlier vigilance evaporated. She was back in the thrall of gravel.

Not every person who develops dementia loses the ability to reflect on feelings, motivations, hopes, fears, or the future. It might be that my mother had never really valued introspection, afraid of what she'd find there, or maybe she just always had other things to attend to. Maybe her situation now was not really that different from what it would have been without the diagnosis of Alzheimer's. But in our discussion of gravel, she was being introspective, much more so than usual. A typical conversation in which I asked her to think about something important usually went something like this:

"Can you think about a situation where you wouldn't feel comfortable living on your own anymore? Like if your memory got worse? Or if you weren't able to do things on your own anymore?"

"Oh, I'm sure I'll need to move into one of those places some day. I know that's coming. But I'm not ready now."

"I know you're not ready now. Can imagine a time when you would be ready?"

"I don't know."

"Well, can we talk about it right now? Can we think about it together?"

"I think I'm fine right now."

"Yes, I think you're fine right now, too. But what kinds of things would let you know you weren't fine? If you couldn't feed yourself? If you couldn't get up and down the stairs?"

"Well I can do all those things just fine."

"Yes, but . . ."

And so on. I wanted to honor my mother's wishes for future care, but to do that, I needed to know what they were. All I could ever really gather was that she thought she was fine; that she was lucky to be in such great health, and that she was ready for a walk.

The "half full" interpretation of my mother's compulsions at this stage was that one, they were heart healthy with all of that walking and deep bending; and two, at least she stuck to a consistent route when she walked on her own. Her caregivers and I took her to parks and forested areas for beauty and variety, but on her own, my mom walked the same two-mile circuit from her house. The path had been ingrained in her muscle memory from all those days of walking to the store with her trusty pink cart and Doozy. Now she walked it alone without the grocery store as a destination but with determination just the same. Perhaps missing the weight of the once familiar cart and dog leash in her hands, she now filled them with new and diverse objects that she found along the way. She still loved white gravel, but on her walks around her neighborhood she found many other treasures, including, and this is by no means a complete list: two moldy Japanese cookbooks, a thick stack of brown paper bags, a black and white knitted purse full of knitted caps and men's t-shirts, a flashlight, a small box of computer cables, empty soda bottles, a broken cell phone, a deflated, parrot-shaped pool toy, dead batteries, cushions for outdoor furniture, rubber bands, a twin-size bed quilt, a sixty pound, plastic, 4'x 4' x 4' dollhouse (presumably carted home with a wheelbarrow?), two pairs of Groucho Marx-like glasses with fake nose, the odd piece of lumber, a bag of children's toys, a 3' x 4' laminated poster a sociology student created to explain bias on match.com, the bottom part of a blue, ele-phant-shaped humidifier, two felted masquerade ball masks, a pair of black running shoes, coils of wire, someone's recycling bin, folders full of medical bills, a pink dildo, a small pot pipe, a five and two ones, cash. Whenever my mom showed me what she'd found, she always said the same thing: "Well, I didn't want to leave it there! It was just lying in the middle of the street!"

The Alzheimer's literature talks about hoarding and rum-maging in the most general terms. People with dementia might hoard items or rummage around in them because they are bored, because they want to protect themselves against future losses, because they worry about things being stolen from them, because are confused about what's worth keeping and what should be thrown away, or because they no longer have control over their own behavior. All of these were true of my mother to greater and lesser degrees. Of course, in some cases the person may have always had a hoarding instinct and the disease just amplifies that tendency. My mother, by contrast, had always had a fairly discriminating eye for what she liked and wanted, and she never tolerated piles or messes, but I wondered if her hoarding had its root cause in her basic frugality and her inability to pass up anything free. Grocery store samples or free trial subscriptions had always appealed to her, but now they were irresistible. In the grocery store, she'd circle back around to the man handing out cheese or the lady giving out yogurt cups two or three times, like a wasp to a soda can, each time delighted with whatever morsel the kind person handed her.

Just as I got used to her fetish for gravel, I got used to finding new objects sitting on her kitchen counter and hearing her familiar explanation: "It was right there in the middle of the street!" It was just stuff. If it gave her pleasure, fine. What got harder to manage was the unpredictability of her coming and going because suddenly our smoothly-running schedule was catching on snags. I got calls from caregivers telling me that my mother wasn't at home, asking if I knew where she was. No, not exactly, I'd admit, but I knew her typical route and would ask them to please drive it slowly till they found her. It wasn't hard. Sometimes I found her when I wasn't even looking, like the time my son and I saw her crossing the grocery store parking lot near where we'd parked to get frozen yogurt. "Do you want some?" we asked casually, to get past her confusion about why we were there. Once on my way home from teaching I saw her picking blackberries, and when I pulled up to her and said "hi," she gave me a sun-blind scowl that morphed into a look half resistant, half surprised. "How did you know I was here?" she asked. "Am I supposed to be somewhere?" I checked my watch. No, she had already been out with a caregiver that morning, had already taken a walk. She was carrying a handful of leaves, a plastic bag full of rocks, bird feathers, and a red, plastic drinking cup filled with blackberries. I talked her into the car and gave her a ride home, not sure that she wouldn't head right back out after I drove away.

Though eventually this neighborhood cruise became part of the new normal in caring for my mother, a lot of "what ifs" came up that were equal parts procedure and worry. What if they couldn't find her? How long should they look? What if they looked, couldn't find her, and waited in her driveway, and she still didn't show up? What then? Trying not to minimize the dangers to my mom or over catastrophize, I suggested a protocol of looking and waiting and calling us, and, if we weren't reachable by phone, calling 9-1-1 if their 2-hour shift was up and she still hadn't come home. That was the first plan I came up with; the second was to research various technologies that might help.

In this age of high-tech, Bourne-identity type gizmos, I thought there'd be an easy solution, maybe something like what a woman I know got for her dogs: collars with built-in cameras that can feed a live stream to her cell phone, along with a GPS signal, to show her exactly where they'd run off to. Only, how would my mom remember to put on such a device? And turn it on? Or what about the Safe Alert type devices, necklaces a person can wear with buttons to press whenever help is needed? But what if the button gets pressed three times a day because the person wearing it wonders what it is? Or doesn't press it at all because they forgot about it? And what about the GPS insoles that you could use to track a person with a computer or smartphone? Great if she only had one pair of shoes and we coordinated our efforts seamlessly to make sure the insoles were recharged at night, when she wouldn't need them, and then had the shoes reassembled every morning. And for any GPS device, what if signals went down, or she wandered behind a concrete wall? What if the system could only alert us to where she was 30 minutes ago? This is not to say I was expecting a fail-safe solution, or that I was, as the saying goes, making perfection the enemy of the good. I just wanted something relatively affordable that that wasn't too much more complicated than the current drive-around-till-you-find-her system we already had in place.

New technologies that will not only be able to track our loved ones' every move, but their general health and well being, are said to be just around the corner. Smart devices will be able to monitor blood pressure, hydration, body temperature, and blood sugar. If I were wondering if my mom had eaten, or if all she'd had was ice cream, I could just login and find out. With the wide range of technological wonders on the horizon and some already in use, I could know if her front door was open, if she left her fireplace on, if her toilet was running, and what she was wearing. Already we have devices that can detect sudden moves, especially sudden vertical descents signaling a fall, so I can imagine a time when similar devices will be able to tell us many more prosaic details, as well. How many times has she gone to the bathroom? What has she seen on television? What words has she uttered? With the assistance of such gizmos' panoptic vision and insight, literally, into a dementia sufferer's daily life, we could, paradoxically, give that person a greater semblance of freedom and autonomy. It sounds a bit grim, I know, like living under house arrest, or being constantly on display, but for my mother, who wanted to stay in her house no matter the cost, such gadgets could be a godsend.

I eventually decided to go with a fairly old-school technology supported by our local Alzheimer's Society. It's called Project Lifesaver, and it requires users to wear a small 1"x 1.5"x 1" radio frequency transmitting device (about the size of two small match boxes glued together, one on top of the other) on a wrist or ankle. The battery inside lasts from 30-60 days and gets changed by someone from the Alzheimer's Society. In my mom's case, they could check it when she went there for her once-a-week "Staying Connected" group. It helps that our community is fairly small and close knit. The man who changes the battery is also the search-and-rescue volunteer who'd help the sheriff's department go out and search for my mom in the event that she went missing, using the radio transmission receiver equipment that would detect her unique signal. They'd start by looking at her last known location then spiral out, looking for the signal that could be detected up to a mile and a half away. The blurb for the device on the Alzheimer's Society website says: "Nationally, the average search time for an Alzheimer's patient drops from twelve hours to about thirty minutes using this technology. When you think of a ninety-pound, eighty-year-old grandmother outside in twenty degree weather in her nightgown, this reduction in search time can easily mean the difference between life and death." I had not been thinking of the dangers to my mom in those terms, given that she had been taking her walks in daylight, fully clothed, but I knew things could change. I knew that the bulky little box on my mom's ankle couldn't keep her from taking a walk at night or wearing the wrong clothes for the weather, but for the time being—after she stopped cutting it off and putting it into her bathroom drawer—it did give us all a little peace of mind.

Around that time we joked that there were really two reasons to call 9-1-1. We might call if my mom went missing, but we began to wonder if people in her neighborhood might call if she kept "finding" so much stuff. Given the sheer volume and quality of the things she brought home, I worried that my mother was not finding things "in the street," as she always swore, but in the backseat of an unlocked car or just inside an open garage door. Living close to student apartments, it's true that she passed many hastily scribbled "free" signs set next to discarded objects that end-of-term renters left out on their curbs, and I'm sure that trash and recycling day also offered up all kinds of temptations. But still, I wondered, could her compulsion to pick stuff up be turning her into a thief?

As if in answer to these unwholesome thoughts about my innocent mother, I received an email from Julia, who always sent reports following her visits with my mom. She wrote that that morning my mother hadn't wanted to go anywhere, but eventually, with a bit of coaxing, my mom had agreed to get dressed and take Julia on her usual neighborhood walk. This was the first time Julia had made the circuit with my mother rather than driving around it looking for her, and she said it was interesting to see the route as my mother saw it and to enter into my mother's realm of expertise. My mother got to be in charge and lead the way. And apparently, according to Julia's report, it was exactly as my mother always said. Things lay in the street waiting to be discovered. "We found a kitchen knife sticking out of the ground along the way," Julia wrote, "and, of course, took it with us."

16 ROOMMATE

Sometimes you have to make changes in how you're giving care by the seat of your pants, responding to a sudden, emergent need. Sometimes you can only make them after long and thoughtful planning, and the change itself—taking away the car, bringing in paid caregivers, moving the person into assisted living—has to occur with SWAT-team like precision. Other times, inspiration strikes, and without any forethought whatsoever, you act.

The day a fellow yoga teacher told me she was thinking about moving to Bellingham, only she wasn't sure where she'd live because she didn't have much money, my muse was on duty. I heard myself say, "Hey! You could live with my mom. In her guest bedroom. For free!" Out of my mouth, the words created for me an image of my mother and Lihwa having an easy rapport as they both came and went according to their schedules, checking in, saying good morning, saying good night. Someone to say goodnight to was what my mother's carefully orchestrated schedule currently lacked. As it was, no one was on duty after 6 p.m., so what my mother did from that hour till the next morning was a mystery. I had no reason to think she'd been doing anything dangerous like going outside or leaving the front door open, but short of seeing for myself, I simply had no idea. I'd been reluctant to call her every night because I didn't want to rouse her if she was already in bed—sometimes as early as 7:30—and I didn't want to risk confusing her, making her think she had to be up and ready to go on an outing. If someone just lived there with her, I thought, not as a caregiver but as a roommate, just another warm body in the three-bedroom house, calls and check-ins wouldn't be necessary. Regular human interaction would suffice.

To see if this could possibly work, I suggested that Lihwa and I go over to my mom's for a casual visit during which I'd set the trap. I knew my mother would reject the idea of a roommate out of hand because she still believed that she was perfectly fine living alone. She still claimed that she shopped for herself and cooked her own meals, and there was no benefit to telling her otherwise. I figured we could present Lihwa's story in such a way that it would get past my mom's "I'm fine" defense mechanism and appeal to her generous nature, that shoulder-patting side of her that genuinely cared about others' well being. Since she had often said what a waste it was to have such a large house for just one person, I thought that if I could get her to think of this whole roommate scheme as her idea, a kind offer that she was making to a lovely young woman in need, it just might work.

The visit went well. We touched on topics dear to my mom's heart, including Lihwa's hair, which my mom unselfconsciously touched and admired; Lihwa's parents, who'd emigrated from China, a subject that got my mom talking about her own childhood migration from Minnesota to Arizona; and the restaurant Lihwa's parents owned that Lihwa worked at several nights a week. That topic gave me the opportunity I needed to lay out the bait. I said, as if in passing, "Lihwa lives with her parents down in Anacortes. When she teaches, she has a 45-minute drive to get here. That's a long way to drive." Lihwa sat in the chair closest to my mom; I sat on the couch across the living room. We exchanged a look and let the words fill the space between us. As if on cue, my mom reached over to Lihwa, patted her knee and said warmly, "You know what? I have a spare bedroom I never use. You could stay here with me. You wouldn't have to pay me anything!" When the visit ended there were smiles all around, hugs, and a fond, "Okay, see you soon!"

At that point on the Alzheimer's journey, my mother's memory was such that an hour after that meeting, nothing remained. I knew not to bring it up as a topic of conversation because I feared that with no memories of the pleasant afternoon to draw on, old attitudes would prevail. "Who? What woman? I don't want someone living here!" Any time we'd visited the topic of my sister moving up from Arizona to live with her—an idea my mom floated out of concern for my sister's financial instability that my sister had always rejected—the conversation began on a positive note but ended with a litany of her fearful projections: she can't smoke in here; she can't bring all those cats; she'd have to clean up after herself; she couldn't leave the TV on all night; I don't know what she likes to eat; I couldn't drive her everywhere; what would she do for work? And so on. To avoid this kind of conversation and its attendant anxiety, I didn't want to raise the topic of Lihwa moving in until we had an actual date in sight. Then, just two days before the move, we started over from the beginning, playing the same parts, hoping for the same results.

Lihwa and I showed up for a casual visit with my mom, sat in the same seats, and had the same conversation, complete with a discussion of hair, Lihwa's parents, her parents' restaurant, and Lihwa's 45-minute drive. Repeat, repeat, repeat. This time, however, my mother didn't take the bait right away, so with just a little more urgency, I said it again. "Isn't that too bad? Lihwa has to drive back and forth, 45 minutes each way." There was the briefest pause, just long enough for me to wonder if I'd seriously misjudged my mother's openness to change and her predictable kindness, before she bent forward, patted Lihwa on the knee, and said, "You know what? I have a spare bedroom I never use. You could stay here with me."

I can't say it went off without a hitch, but few things on the dementia journey do. Lihwa was only going to stay four nights a week, arriving Tuesday evening and going back to stay at her parents' house on the weekend. On the first two nights of her stay at my mom's, she didn't come in until after 8:30 p.m., which is by no means late for a 33-year-old, but past my 78-year-old mom's bedtime. So much for having someone there to say goodnight. Then on Thursday afternoon of that first week, when Lihwa was happy to spend a little time visiting, my mom exchanged a few strained words with her then bolted. Katie, the caregiver who was on the schedule to spent time with my mom that afternoon, found my mom walking toward my house, presumably to complain, and successfully cajoled and distracted her for her two-hour shift. As soon as she returned my mom to her house, however, where a bewildering silky-haired stranger kept trying to make small talk, my mother headed right back out again. Dressed in black from head to toe, she made it to my house, in the dark, carrying a stack of file folders and manila envelopes she'd paused long enough to lift out of someone's recycling bin along the way. She wanted to ask me who that woman was, why she was in her house, and how long she planned to stay.

It didn't seem like an auspicious start. Wasn't my rule of thumb for caregivers that they had to ease the burden, not increase it? I worried I'd made a horrible mistake. But by Friday afternoon of the second week, when Lihwa joined us in the kitchen and regaled my mom and her house-call-making hair-cutter with stories about seeing the Seahawks in Super Bowl XLVIII, I congratulated myself on the plan's success. I could tell that my mom, sitting there with a towel around her shoulders and curlers in her hair, waiting for her perm to take hold, had no idea who or what the Seahawks were or what Lihwa's number 12 jersey meant, but she enjoyed the friendly energy. After that, I stopped hearing complaints, or anything else about Lihwa at all, so I chose to interpret no news as good news and watched my mother settle into yet another new normal.

As I told people about the arrangement, especially people who had regular contact with my mom, I got nothing but kudos. So many and with such enthusiasm that I began to think that maybe they knew something I didn't. When the program leader at the Alzheimer's Society told me what a great idea she thought it was, for obvious safety reasons, then proceeded to tell me about a man suffering from dementia who didn't know how to get himself out of his burning house, I left off feeling self-congratulatory and started to ask myself if I had been— and still was—living with my head in the sand. Could my mom survive an emergency at home? Would she know what to do in a fire?

Lately it had become apparent that she didn't know the word "microwave" any more and couldn't use the new one we'd just bought her. She kept dismantling the flushing apparatus in her upstairs toilet, had been using a vacuum cleaner without a bag to catch the dust, and she had somehow moved a 200-pound, potted blue spruce from her driveway into her garage. One could see that she didn't always make the best decisions. Would she know how to call 9-1-1 or walk over to a neighbor's house to ask for help? I asked her matter-of-factly if she knew what she'd do in the event of a fire, but calm was not the proper testing ground. How could I anticipate what her reflexes would be in a crisis? I fantasized about staging a few fake emergencies to see what would happen. Could I blow smoke into her house and watch through the windows to see what she did? An off-and-on roommate was no guarantee of her safety. Maybe having Lihwa stay at my mom's house four nights a week wasn't so much an extra dose of care but an insufficient band aid on a gaping wound. With only a twinge of paranoia I imagined Adult Protective Services paying me a visit, asking me how and when I planned to give my mother better care. Asking me, didn't I know she no longer knew how to use a microwave? That her toilet was broken? That her house was dusty, and that she was likely to give herself a hernia with all that heavy lifting? What kind of daughter was I to let such an impaired mother continue to live alone? Did the roommate situation really change anything?

For the two months it lasted, it went well, but then it ended. I could have foreseen it, and I might have asked more questions going into it in the first place. But I understood. Lihwa was young and untethered, her teaching schedule changed, and she liked to travel. She wasn't looking for a committed relationship, at least not with my mother.

The roommate experiment didn't last long, but it didn't disturb anything. It didn't, as my mother had begun saying, "get her all tangled up."

The only change that I could see in those last few months, apart from the comings and goings of Lihwa, was that my mom had added an occasional detour into Fred Meyer on her regular walks. I knew this because I confiscated a $10 gift card she'd apparently earned for pushing a cart back to the store from where it had been left in a field, and because one day I saw her there. I'd been driving her route looking for her, and then, after seeing her crossing the parking lot away from the store entrance carrying a small red bag, I stopped to watch from across the street. Seeing the bag, I went into a slight panic: had she been collecting gift cards all along, and was she back to buying beer? Did she, with or without meaning to, steal something? Had she been helped in the store by dementia-friendly clerks, or had she wandered through without raising anyone's concerns?

Idling in the mobile home park across the street, feeling part voyeur, part private eye, I tried to see her with less anxiety and more compassion. There was my mother, making the most of what she had. No purse, no shopping cart, no schedule. No one to go home to. Who, seeing her in the parking lot, would even know that she had Alzheimer's? And what would anyone feel compelled to do if they did? Did she look unsafe or acutely alone? She was simply walking across the parking lot, smiling, carrying a red, plastic bag.

I watched her cross the street at the cross walk, where she knew to press the button to activate the signal, and I saw her get close to my car, where she tried to wave me on, saying, "You go on; I can go behind you." Only when I rolled down the window to wave and say hello did she recognize me and give her customary, startled response: "How did you find me? Am I supposed to be somewhere?" From that independent-seeming older woman walking home from the grocery store, she morphed back into my mother, dependent and demented, but still smiling. She had been fine out on her own, taking a walk and cruising through Fred Meyer, but she was also fine getting into the car and letting me set the terms for the rest of the afternoon. She had grown mostly easy, mostly compliant. Her red bag, I noticed, as she buckled herself into her seat, had no stolen merchandise in it but was instead filled with fall-colored leaves and pinecones.

17. ARE WE THERE YET?

In the 8-limbed yoga practice I study and teach, I have learned that the journey and the destination are one. The word "yoga," from its Sanskrit root *"yug,"* means "to yoke" or "join," and the 8th and last limb of the practice is *Samadhi*, which is commonly translated as "enlightenment" but also suggests "integration." So from the very moment we start to do yoga, we are already yoking or unifying, bringing things together, which, paradoxically, is also supposed to free us up. According to one translation of the philosophy that modern yoga often draws on, the enlightened yogi lives in *dharma megha Samadhi*, or "unsurpassed bliss," free from time, place, and space—"while others remain trapped in this net."

As I continue to care for my mother, I often wonder which of us is trapped and which of us is free. She is clearly the one liberated from the demands of the calendar, never knowing if my son is in school or on summer vacation, if the trees don't have leaves because it's not spring yet or because we're heading into winter. Neither is she slave to the clock. During our short winter days, 3 p.m. feels like midnight to her, and on days when she happens to get out of bed early, 9 a.m. feels like late afternoon. On a larger scale, she can't believe she's 78; she can't believe my son turned 17; she can't remember that her father died about 40 years ago. Memories of place are beginning to escape her now, too. Recently she told her family's migration story but had them moving to California instead of Arizona.

But she remains more solidly rooted in her house than ever. Every day she tells me how much she loves living there, and every day I see evidence that despite its inherent risks, it is a space that engages and enriches her. She changes the decorations on her mantle piece on a daily basis, moves house plants around, and stuffs drawers full of the junk she can't bear to get rid of. On most days she sweeps every single leaf off her front porch and driveway, and she spends a good amount of time going in and out, calling for the cat who's usually standing right behind her. I know she gets frustrated and often feels bereft by all that she's lost, but as I shuffle her here and there with an eye on the clock, thinking about her schedule, making sure I have someone for the next shift, wondering about her next meal, imagining the next thing that could go wrong, I do often think that despite all my hours on the yoga mat, my mother is much closer to *dharma megha Samadhi* than I am.

I remind myself that it wasn't always so. The accounts I have recorded here give evidence. At times she was miserable and angry; there were times when not knowing what day or season it was confused and depressed her. As I note this seeming change for the better in her spirits and outlook, I could try to congratulate myself on helping get her to this point. But nothing is clear. At what I am calling this halfway mark, when my mother has lived ten years past the time she first recognized that something was wrong with her memory, six years past a diagnosis, I still wonder what my role on this journey is. I know that what I do makes much of her routine as well as her freedom possible, but I am not sure what to think about it. I have my mantras, but are those serving me, primarily, or her? Am I a caregiver or a care manager? Am I a dutiful daughter?

Or am I, having written this book, a somewhat complaining one? Not knowing what's ahead and what more will be demanded of me in terms of time, attention, and resources, how can I say anything definitive about what it means to care for a parent through Alzheimer's? It might still go horribly wrong. But if I wait and only tell these stories from a distant end point, I fear that the truth and vitality of the present moment, even the spark given off by not knowing, will be lost. Again I find that the language of caring for a person with Alzheimer's and the language of yoga overlap. In the epilogue to his *Wisdom of Patanjali's Yoga Sutras*, Ravi Ravindra writes:

> Wonder requires a state of unknowing—not a state of ignorance, but of innocence in which one is free from knowledge, known, knower and the need to know. Then sometimes one is connected with a quality of awareness in which the Mystery is still not solved, and it has no publicly communicable logical answer, but it is dissolved. This Mystery no longer troubles one or makes one apprehensive or anxious; it does not evoke a denial or a rejection. (177)

I feel far from the place where the Mystery is dissolved, and I can still feel quite apprehensive about all that lies ahead, both for my mother and for myself, but I can say that I am well past denial, and almost past the urge to argue. Almost. Some habits are hard to break.

It has always struck me as deeply ironic that I switched over from teaching technical writing at a university to teaching yoga—a practice that requires less by way of precision and more in the way of general awareness—at about the same time my mother started losing her memory. Technical writing is all about documenting what is known, for a specific group of knowers, for a very precise need to know, while yoga asks that practitioners stay present to what is happening in the moment and move away, when possible, from labels and narratives that concretize past experiences or future possibilities. Technical writing is not interested in mysteries. It seeks, first and foremost, to communicate logical answers.

While the Iyengar Yoga method I am immersed in does have an eye on precision for alignment and explanation, its larger goal is to get people to start fresh every day, experiencing whatever is going on in the body, mind, and soul without trying to nail it down for keeps. Unfortunately, just because I switched career paths, I couldn't swap out my basic orientation to the world. I brought my fact-finding self to the work of caregiving out of lifelong habit. It has been a struggle to switch mental tracks and bring the more yogic goal of staying present to caring for my mom, even though my mom is a daily reminder—what with her fascination for white gravel, leaves, and pine cones—that the present moment can be full of pleasant surprises, over and over again. Because walking together is something we can still enjoy, I get to practice softening into her simple enjoyment of life several times a week. "Practice is not performance," I tell my students. I have to tell myself that, too.

Now when we walk together on forest paths with any kind of incline, my mom routinely asks, "Are we getting close to the top?" Most of the trails we walk now meander here and there with a few ups and downs, but we typically avoid the steep ones that have a peak, let alone a sweeping vista. Usually we're on a fairly level or mildly undulating path.

When she asks me if we're close to the top, I wonder what her body is telling her, how she's reading the gentle ascents and their paired descents. Is she having a harder time breathing? Do her knees ache? I often think she must be remembering Squaw Peak, the stark desert mountain she climbed regularly when she lived in Phoenix that had a top so obvious it had poles and chains to help people pull themselves up the steep, final steps. She had a similarly steep hill she liked to hike when she lived near San Luis Obispo, California. You knew you were done when there was nowhere else to go and everything lay below you. I wonder if she is disappointed at the end of our walks when there is no "there" there, no final ascent or "hurray, we made it" kind of moment. I think she likes those. An obvious "top" to our walks would help her know where she was, if only for a few minutes. The constant ups and downs leave her feeling a bit lost, and she'll often say, "If I didn't have you here with me, I wouldn't know which way to go."

And so, her dependence on me is also my reward. I am her guide. She trusts me, and I show up for her with all my own repetitious baggage. I love my mother, and lately, more than ever, she makes me laugh. Recently she gave a birthday card to my husband, five months away from the actual day, signed, "Your bossy sister-in-law." One evening I gave her the task of pulling Italian parsley leaves off their stems, and she was so diligent and attentive that she came over to show me one single leaf that looked more like curly parsley than flat, and she asked me what to do with that "stranger." She can make jokes about her radio tracking device, saying that after she's dead it'll still be blinking. Yet finding moments of kinship and connection through this process remains complicated. As a caregiver, you watch the person you're caring for differently than the way a child generally has to experience a parent. Children not responsible for a parent's care can listen dispassionately to whatever their parent is up to and then get back to their own lives. Being responsible changes everything. While the demands of caregiving pull me closer to the details of my mother's life— what she does with her time, where she is at any given moment, what she is or isn't eating, what she is or isn't drinking— those same demands drive a wedge into the heart of our mother-daughter relationship.

A few years ago, the similarities my mother and I share, the inevitable biological likenesses we have—similar kneecaps, same history of uterine fibroids, a shared taste in literature— started to feel a little claustrophobic. Genetics may only play a small part in determining who gets the later-onset form of the disease, but who has a parent with Alzheimer's who hasn't asked, "Will this be me?" You'd think asking that question would initiate a karmic consciousness that would immediately make me an excellent caregiver, that I would instinctively jump to the "as you sow, so shall you reap" law of cause and effect and transform myself into Mother Theresa. Instead, it has made me watch myself obsessively for all the ways I might be following in my mother's footsteps. It makes me nervous every time a well-meaning store clerk says, "I can tell you two are related!" Like mother, not like daughter, has become a more paranoid mantra. I will admit that part of me believes, quite superstitiously and irrationally, that if I do the opposite of what my mother did at various junctures in her life, I can avoid her fate. No hysterectomy, no divorce, not so much alcohol. Where she now walks stiffly, holding her arms straight down by her sides, I remind myself to swing my arms in time with my legs. Where she looks into the sun with a squint that makes her seem angry, I try to always wear sunglasses. So imagine my dismay when I catch myself standing next to my mother, talking with strangers on the trail or looking out her kitchen window, and I notice that we're striking the exact same pose: arms hanging down from softly rounded shoulders, the right hand cupped over the left, fingers curled over each other. I see myself as her carbon copy and jerk my hands apart and put them awkwardly on my hips. Or the times I stare up at the sky and say, "Look at those clouds!" and my son says, "You sound like Grandma." Or when I catch myself saying, in response to a complicated or nuanced explanation, "Oh. That's nice," just like my mom does because "nice" is so much easier than anything else. Ruts worn deep by nature and nurture are hard not to fall into, or, once there, crawl out of. I work at keeping steady on my own path and feel an odd mixture of guilt and pity when I hear someone at support group say, "This will be my first day off in a year." I think, "See? What do I have to complain about?" followed by, "How can you stand it? You need to get away!"

But for all my pushing away and claiming my own necessary space, there is no question that I am my mother's daughter, and that for better and worse, we walk this path together, round and round and round. But only one of us is stopping to pick up rocks and leaves. "Don't wait for me," she still says. "I'll catch up." I have to force myself to repeat the easiest mantra of all, the hardest one to practice: patience, patience, patience. And then I wonder about my mother's words. Is she going to catch up to me, or should I be the one catching up to her?

EPILOGUE

As I ready this manuscript for publication, much has changed, but my mother is still alive and still doing relatively well. We still walk together, though more slowly and with less ambition. She still has her physical and conversational loop de loops, like picking up leaves and asking me "how are the boys?" every few minutes, and I have my many repetitive behaviors and phrases, like trying to slow my breath with deep, full inhalations and long steady exhalations, and saying with as much cheerfulness as I can muster, "I'm going now, but I'll see you soon."

"Tomorrow?" she asks.

"Soon," I say.

I still lie when I have to, but I tell the truth when I can.

I consider my mother somewhere in the middle of her journey because of her strong physical health, but she is beginning to lose language and starting to enter a more disordered reality. She wonders why her parents don't visit or call, for example, and she talks about what she'll do when she graduates from high school. She wonders if she should start applying for jobs. She asks my son, Wilson, "Do you know Wilson?" and doesn't detect the humor in his voice when he answers, "Yeah, he's a pretty cool kid."

Since finishing the last chapter of this book, we have gone through a few more painful transitions along the stair-step decline of Alzheimer's and caregiving, but I know we still have a ways to go. Along the way I have picked up a new mantra practice, a 12-minute exercise called Kirtan Kriya, that is supposed to be good for cognition. Repetition in this practice, like in so many others, seems to help keep me grounded, which in turn keeps me present for my mother.

I thank, again, all the wonderful support I've received along the way from my husband and son, my support group, the programs and resources available to me in Bellingham, my extended family, and all my friends who kindly ask after my mother and always tell me to give her their best wishes, even though she won't know who they're from. I thank my first reader, Lisa Holt, as well.

Writing has been a great comfort also, so maybe, after the rest of this journey plays out, I will repeat myself in this most constructive way and write the rest of my mother's and my story. Until then, interested readers can find photos and weekly updates on our journey at an online photo blog: https://www.blipfoto.com/dwbham.

ABOUT THE AUTHOR

Denise Weeks lives with her husband and Corgi in Bellingham, Washington. The teenager has been launched. She is a Certified Iyengar Yoga Teacher, copyeditor, and caregiver.